SUSTAINABLE SPIRITUALITY

MAINTAINING FAITH IN THE FACE OF ADVERSITY

BY S. RICHARD NELSON

First Edition published August 2016

ISBN-13: 978-0-9904973-0-1
ISBN-10: 0990497305

Broken Hill Publications
Glenwood Springs, Colorado

www.sustainabilitygodsway.com

Cover Design by: Connie Gorton

"Peace I leave with you, my peace I give unto you: not as the world giveth, give I unto you. Let not your heart be troubled, neither let it be afraid."

John 14:27 (KJV)

Contents

This book is lovingly dedicated to
my beautiful wife, Connie,
who provided not only the idea for the book
but also, through her Christ-like example,
the inspiration for me to write it.

PREFACE

The fundamental principle of Christianity is faith in the Lord Jesus Christ. We accept Him as our Lord and Savior and look forward to the time when he returns to reign as King of kings. The second coming of Christ is mentioned over 1,500 times in the Old Testament and over 300 times in the New Testament. It has often been prophesied that the time of the Second Coming will be a time of pessimism and fear, discouragement and despair.

Luke describes the prevailing conditions in the last days as a time of "signs in the sun and the moon and the stars, and on the earth nations will be in distress, anxious over the roaring of the sea and the surging waves. People will be fainting from fear and from the expectation of what is coming on the world, for the powers of the heavens will be shaken."[1]

Today we cautiously watch as humanity's structures begin to crumble. Global alliances are strained as political turmoil runs rampant. The war on terror does little to stop terrorism yet continues to cost precious lives. From commerce to health care, from fiscal policies to food production, our society is falling apart.

Marriage is assailed and attacked and more than half end in divorce. Children are viewing pornography, taking drugs and alcohol, becoming pregnant before graduating high school.

The world's privileged few buy summer homes in the south of France while nearly a billion others around the world face starvation. We

---

[1] Luke 21:25,26 (NET).

question the morality of how some people "own pennies in a jar" while others "own oil tankers." We deliberate over why "some spend winter in a palace; some spend it in blankets." [2]

And so we send out bell ringers at Christmas time and set up yard sales to raise money to feed the poor, clean the air, save the latest endangered species, or whatever the most recent popular cause is. We develop programs to provide birth control in high school and set up daycare services for students. We offer no-fault, low-cost divorce so that everyone can participate. We mount massive drug awareness education programs and expand our drug rehabilitation centers all the while we fight to legalize recreational drug use. We are applying a Band-Aid® to a gaping, open wound while slashing our wrists all at the same time.

These are not sustainable solutions to society's dilemmas. They address symptoms of the

---

[2] From *Get Up Off Our Knees*, by The Housematins, London 0 Hull 4, 1986.

disease and not the disease itself. We are merely hacking away at the weeds but leaving the roots of sin firmly in place beneath the soil.

Paul warned us that "in the last days difficult times will come. For people will be lovers of themselves, lovers of money, boastful, arrogant, blasphemers, disobedient to parents, ungrateful, unholy, unloving, irreconcilable, slanderers, without self-control, savage, opposed to what is good, treacherous, reckless, conceited, loving pleasure rather than loving God. They will maintain the outward appearance of religion but will have repudiated its power." [3] Well, that pretty much sums up our day and times!

But there is a solution. It requires a return to the Spirit of Truth. It requires replacing Jesus Christ and his teachings in our society, in our government, in our schools and, most especially, in our own hearts and minds.

---

[3] 2 Timothy 3: 1-5 (NET).

Why is it necessary that we center our confidence, our hope, and our trust in the one solitary figure of Jesus of Nazareth? Why is faith in him so necessary to peace of mind in this life and hope in the world to come? And how do we avoid getting caught up in the prevailing pessimism and fatalism of the last days?

Our answers to these questions will determine whether we face the future with sustainable spirituality that will give us courage, hope, and optimism or whether, with the rest of the world, we fall into apprehension, anxiety, and despair.

I know there are many who do not believe in God and regard religion as nothing more than fantasy and fallacy. They are convinced that humanity can, on its own, surmount the world's troubles and fix the problems of society through its own resourcefulness and ingenuity. But they are building their houses on sand. And God cannot continue to withhold the prophesied cataclysm that comes as a consequence of sin.

In turbulent and troubling times, the Christian pathway can seem almost too tough to travel. How do we maintain our feet on the footholds on faith as the prophesied future unfolds? If we regard Christianity as nothing more than a bundle of beliefs and behaviors we painstaking carry on our shoulders, it could definitely appear overwhelming.

But for the disciples of Christ who are spiritually prepared to sustain their belief and maintain their faith, their devotion becomes not a burden but a blessing. Christianity is not a weight on their shoulders but, rather, wings on their backs. It brings light in dark times and sweetens the bitter cup of adversity. It sustains them in the flaming furnace of fear and comforts them in the deep pits of despair. Christianity is the assurance of a qualified Captain on the very rough voyage of life.

The Christian pathway is the comforting assurance of an everlasting light which shines in the darkest night and an eternal warmth felt within the loneliest heart. This is the power of that sustainable hope which is provided as a gift to all of us through the pure love of Christ.

The purpose of this book is to help us look carefully and honestly into our own lives to prevent the development of any spiritual infirmity which could destroy our faith, particularly in light of the warnings that have been given to us about the last days. It is a call to prepare ourselves for the day when all of society's houses that have been built on sand will come tumbling down around us.

But as we reposition our lives to be closer to God, he will become closer to us and we will develop even greater spiritual sustainability through increased faith in Christ. Sustainable spirituality intensifies as we follow Christ's teachings.

Jesus clearly taught: "I am the way, and the truth, and the life. No one comes to the Father except through me." [4]

He did not just bring light into a darkened and fallen world; Jesus is the light.

He did not simply show us the way; Jesus is the way.

He didn't just teach truth; Jesus is the truth.

He did not merely make the resurrection available; Jesus is the resurrection and the life.

The greatest benefit and blessing to this world would be for men and women everywhere to practice the pure love of Christ. Christ's pure love is simple kindness. It is humility and patience. It is a selfless love that asks nothing in return. It does not tolerate evil or delight in sin. It condemns ridicule, vulgarity and abuse. A heart filled with Christ's love has no

---

[4] John 14:6.

place for bigotry, hatred, or violence. It encourages diverse people to live together in Christian love regardless of religious belief, race, nationality, financial standing, education, or culture.

The pure love of Christ will fortify us to sustain our faith and spirituality even through the toughest tribulations and turmoil. Our hope for peace and happiness in this world and for eternal glory hereafter are intrinsically tied to our Lord and Savior, Jesus Christ, the Hope of Israel.

CHAPTER ONE

THE FORGOTTEN SIDE OF SUSTAINABILITY

Sustainable is one of the popular terms currently being tossed about in today's social salad with the intent of educating us on creating a more conscientious way of living. Sustainability relates to a strategy taken by the present population aimed at not diminishing the expectations of future populations to enjoy similar levels of consumption, wealth, utility, or welfare.

In environmental science, sustainability is the capability to survive and endure; it is how biological systems continually remain diverse and productive.

One definition of the word sustainable is *to keep in existence; to maintain*. I like this definition. It is concise and to the point. As a rule, sustainability is simply the endurance of systems and processes.

Sustainable living has become a social challenge that has taken on many forms. Restructured living conditions have created ecovillages and sustainable cities. Adjustments in trade and industry have given us sustainable agriculture and architecture. Science continues to develop "greener" technologies and more renewable energy sources. Individuals around the world are constantly making lifestyle changes to conserve our natural resources.

The prevalent global attention given to sustainability focuses primarily on the physical environment. The predominant issues of environmental degradation, climate change, overconsumption, population growth and society's pursuit of open-ended economic growth in a closed system are not going to be easily mended under the current practices of materialistic self-indulgence, science-based skepticism and political radicalism.

Despite the increased popularity in the use of the term "sustainability," the likelihood that human societies will attain environmental sustainability continues to be in question. Very little attention, however, is given to the spiritual aspects of sustainability without which the world floats rudderless on an angry sea of cataclysmic disasters and exceptional challenges that daily threaten to overwhelm us.

Throughout the world a growing anxiety and fear pervade humanity. For some of us this fear and anxiety may seem increasingly close at hand, but for many others, these heart-troubling emotions are already a constant, persistent and foreboding presence. This constraining fear does not come from the hazards of our circumstances but from the failure of the human heart as it becomes separated from its spiritual nature.

Natural disasters have occurred with increasing regularity in recent years—devastating earthquakes have leveled cities in numerous parts of the world; great storms and hurricanes have ravaged towns and shorelines; damaging and deadly floods have washed through Europe, Asia and the Americas. Major storms seriously affect transportation and food supplies. We continually see reports of long lines at grocery stores as victims of natural disasters try to purchase food supplies and drinkable water.

Other signs of the times include political, social, and economic events that likewise test our spiritual sustainability in distinct ways. Economic instability is commonplace today. We witness disheartening recessions and extensive unemployment, demoralizing depressions and skyrocketing inflation—any of which can be as disastrous as a major earthquake. War and widespread terrorism are becoming the norm in many countries.

It doesn't always take a natural or man-made disaster to test a person's spiritual stability. Even normal daily living can seriously test the parameters of our physical, mental, emotional, and spiritual health. The prophet Moses wrote in his time of the "terror within" and the "sword without" destroying a nation not grounded on a spiritual foundation: "They are a nation devoid of wisdom, and there is no understanding among them. I wish that they were wise and could understand this, and that they could comprehend what will happen to them." [5]

The shepherds "were absolutely terrified" when the angel appeared to them to announce Jesus' birth. So much so that the angel consoled them with the words, "do not be afraid." [6] Jesus ended his earthly ministry telling his apostles: "Peace I leave with you; my peace I give to you; I do not give it to

---

[5] Deuteronomy 32:25, 28-29 (NET).
[6] Luke 2:9-10 (NET).

you as the world does. Do not let your hearts be distressed or lacking in courage." [7]

How can we, as faithful Christians, remain perfectly calm and serene among all the convulsions of the earth—the turmoil, strife, war, pestilence, famine and distress of nations? How do we "keep in existence" our faith? How do we "maintain" our level of spiritually, sustain our peace and not allow our hearts to "be distressed or lacking in courage?"

We knew beforehand that such things would transpire on Earth. We understand the meaning behind these events and view them in their true light. In the Bible God tells us what is going to happen so that we can prepare for and live through these upsetting times without a loss of faith. It is through our knowledge and understanding of Biblical prophecies that the largest portion of our personal preparation rests.

---

[7] John 14:27 (NET).

There are three critical areas of personal preparation that will assist believing Christians to face the distress of troubling times with faith, courage and hope:

1. Knowledge and understanding of world events,

2. physical provision and readiness, and

3. spiritual preparation.

Each one of us should be responsible for our own mental, physical (including economic) and spiritual sustainability.

A Knowledge of World Events

The judgments that will precede the coming of Christ will have a profound effect upon the nations of the world. Great changes are taking place around the world. For those watching (not with physical eyes but with eyes of faith), things that make newspaper headlines or the evening news are seen as partial fulfillment, at least, of events prophesied centuries ago. The only way we can recognize the hand of God in all these happenings is to keep informed of world events and know what is going on around us.

Jesus declared to his disciples over two millennia ago that "this gospel of the kingdom will be preached throughout the whole inhabited earth as a testimony to all the nations, and then the end will come." [8] With the advent of radio, television, the internet and social media, we have seen this prophecy fulfilled in our lifetime. As certainly as this prophecy has been fulfilled, God's purposes will continue to unfold to our view if we have eyes that see and minds that know and understand.

One pivotal step we can take to prepare ourselves for the Second Coming is to gain greater knowledge and understanding. Some of that knowledge will come to us as we read and study God's word. But we must also be educated and knowledgeable about the world around us and the arising events that are part of his magnificent plan

---

[8] Matthew 24:14 (NET).

leading up to the return of his Son to reign as King of kings.

Physical Provision and Readiness

There are five distinct areas in which we need to develop our personal sustainability practices. They are:

1. Education,

2. Employment,

3. Health,

4. Survival Preparedness, and

5. Financial Management.

Before God's final judgments transpire, our personal sustainability could be extensively strained and tested. If we have properly prepared ourselves, then our hearts need not be distressed or lacking in courage. We can then reliably receive the peace that Christ offers us.

Physical provision and readiness will be vital to our personal sustainability in the turbulent times to come. We could easily become isolated and cut-off from customary methods of transportation, business, and community connections. Recent natural disasters have demonstrated that the current infrastructures supporting our day-to-day living are extremely fragile and complex.

With even a minor earthquake, freeway overpasses could collapse, disrupting the flow of traffic in and out of a city. Food and other needed commodities would be unable to reach the marketplaces. Just a single incident like that can put an entire city into crisis with little or no warning. The growing threat of local terrorism can bring widespread social disruption and could restrict a whole population from the usual avenues of provision and protection.

We have become cripplingly dependent on our current social structure for the normal functioning of our lives but may soon find ourselves separated from the usual pattern of society which provides so many of our daily needs.

Spiritual Preparation

Spiritual preparation in a time of crisis is by far the most important and critical aspect of our personal sustainability. When we find ourselves living in economic, political, and spiritual instability—unmistakable indications that Christ's coming is imminent—we need not be troubled.

"Peace I leave with you.... Do not let your hearts be distressed or lacking in courage." [9]

Regrettably, in many cases, our spiritual sustainability is the most neglected aspect of our personal preparation.

During a recent drought in the western United States when hardly any snow or rain had fallen throughout December, local news stations reported the possibility of severe water shortages if

_____

[9] John 14:27 (NET).

circumstances did not improve. The reaction in Colorado and its surrounding states was noteworthy. One news report indicated that wheat shipments out of Idaho jumped from one truck load per week to an astonishing three truck loads per day! The purchase of food storage supplies increased 800 percent that month. Many secured loans and mortgages on property to pay for their emergency food supplies.

People took the threat to their physical provision and readiness very seriously but, during that same time, was there a concurrent rise in the concern over spiritual sustainability? Was there an 800 percent increase in prayer during that same time? Did Bible reading increase significantly that month? Was there a considerable increase in church attendance?

We hurried to stock up on our physical supplies. Did we also hurriedly turn to our God with an increased desire to strengthen and fortify our spiritual sustainability?

We do not know when the calamities and troubles of the last days will fall upon us. The Lord has withheld from us the day and hour of his coming. He simply tells us to watch and be ready. As Christians we must prepare, watch and wait. There are no guarantees in this life except the guarantee of accepting Christ and living righteously.

We can increase our spiritual sustainability and better prepare for the second coming by gaining greater knowledge and understanding of world events; by becoming self-reliant in physical provisions and readiness; and by increasing our spirituality. As we continually strive to improve our spiritual sustainability, we will gain an increased perception of the Lord's promise: "Peace I leave with you; my peace I give to you; I do not give it to you as the world does. Do not let your hearts be distressed or lacking in courage." [10]

If we experience any anxiety over the day of vengeance when the Lord will return, we should let

[10] John 14:27 (NET).

our anxiety be centered on the sanctification of our hearts, the purifying of our desires, and on preparing for the events that are rushing toward us. We must seek to have the Spirit of Christ as we prepare for the days ahead.

CHAPTER TWO

SUSTAINABLE SPIRITUALITY GOALS

Sustainable Development Goals (known as SDGs) are recommended objectives that relate to future global development. The SDGs replaced the Millennium Development Goals (MDGs) which expired at the end of 2015. The MDGs, established in 2000, were adopted by the 189 United Nations member states and more than twenty international organizations.

These goals were created to advance the following sustainable development criteria by 2015:

1. To eradicate extreme poverty and hunger.

2. To achieve universal primary education.

3. To promote gender equality and empower women.

4. To reduce child mortality.

5. To improve maternal health.

6. To combat HIV/AIDS, malaria, and other diseases.

7. To ensure environmental sustainability.

8. To develop a global partnership for development.

According to the data submitted to the United Nations, Cuba was the only nation in the world in 2006 that met the definition of sustainable development.

Similar to sustainable development, achieving sustainable spirituality is not something that happens automatically either. We need to have spiritual goals that advance us along the path of sustainable spirituality. The path of spiritual development is, for the most part, a difficult, uphill effort. We may experience a burst of faith momentarily, then run up against a personal setback somewhere along the way. Doubts arise that could leave us spiritually debilitated.

The demands and responsibilities of our jobs consume our time and distract us from spiritual matters. We become separated from the saving doctrines of Jesus. We allow "little" sins to stunt our spiritual development. It is a continuous struggle to grasp ideals that seldom remain clear and in constant focus, but our efforts to develop sustainable spiritual goals will be blessed by God.

Spirituality doesn't just happen to us. It doesn't simply appear as we get older or more mature. Our good wishes or even excellent church attendance won't, by themselves, create it for us. More is required of us. The development of sustainable spirituality is a personal, volitional effort to understand and carry out the will of God in our lives.

Our willingness to make the effort to set our spiritual development goals is an essential step toward spiritual sustainability. This is a proactive process. It requires desiring and planning with consistency and integrity. It requires escaping from our culturally acquired custom of spending our time and energy on pursuits that provide instantaneous and glamorous worldly rewards. The driving force behind material motivation is immediate gratification and, consequently, spiritual values take a back seat to profits and pleasures.

These cultural habits are dangerous adversaries to sustainable spirituality. Spiritual ideals always run contrary to the purpose and practicality of our pressing worldly values and pursuits. Meaningful truth, whether spiritual or secular, rarely reveals its cherished mysteries to the impatient or impulsive inquirer.

So how do we nurture sustainable spirituality when the influences of the world conspire to confuse, divert and distract us? The answer lies in our ability to build a sustainable spiritual lifestyle founded on solid rock and not on sand.

At times we may feel incapable or ineffectual at furthering our spiritual development. But the trials of today prepare us for the triumphs of tomorrow. Think about that for a minute. Preparation is a present-day pursuit.

So often we imagine that preparation relates more to some intense test we will undergo someday. Through years of education we prepare for the challenge of finding and keeping a job. We even take classes to prepare for childbirth. We purchase emergency supply kits in the event of some future calamity—a flood, an earthquake, a terrorist attack, the loss of employment. We pray and study the Bible to strengthen our faith in Jesus as a means to prepare for the difficulties and distresses of the prophesied future, a time when our faith may be all we have left to rely on.

Spiritual preparation is much more than simply getting ready for the future. The severe hardships ahead may or may not materialize during our lifetime. Of course, we hope that they won't, no matter how much preparation we have undertaken. But a life focused solely on the future disregards and undermines the blessings of the present that make life and living worthwhile today. Spiritual preparation is more about who we become in the present as we plan and prepare for the future.

The exquisite promise of preparation was perceptively explained by Jesus to his apostles on the night he was to be crucified: "Don't let your heart be troubled. You believe in God. Believe also in me. In my Father's house are many mansions. If it weren't so, I would have told you. I am going to prepare a place for you. If I go and prepare a place for you, I will come again, and will receive you to myself; that where I am, you may be there also. Where I go, you know, and you know the way." [11]

Jesus has been patiently and continually preparing the way for our spiritual development and growth. He has gone before us and, even now, he has a place prepared for us in the mansions of his Father. Jesus reaffirms for us that we "know the way." He has so much incredible conviction and certainty in our spiritual sustainability! If our faith in ourselves is ever lacking or diminished, surely we can lean on his faith in us for the time being.

Paul tells us that we should fit our feet with the preparation that comes from the good news of peace. [12] The gospel of Christ engenders peace. Even when it is difficult to follow, when it stretches us to our limits and makes us work harder than we would like, it still creates peace. With peace in our hearts, we are better prepared for anything.

---

[11] John 14:1-4 (WEB).
[12] See Ephesians 6:15.

In this life we think only one thought at a time. Each thought is a choice. According to author Steven Claysen, we think about 50,000 thoughts a day. [13] With this many thoughts running through our heads each day, we certainly have some serious choices to make.

Each day thousands of good choices are presented to us. We could decide to clean out the garage or spend the time studying for a college exam. We might decide to do some much needed yardwork or we might forego all that and just go to lunch with a friend. These are all good, positive choices. But in the final analysis, we must still make the choice. We live only in the present moment; not in the past and not in the future.

My wife, Connie, recently experienced a situation that exemplifies the approach we should take in our spiritual preparation. She sustained an injury to her shoulder that required physical

---

[13] Claysen, Steven, *The Power of Attraction*, White Horse Library, 2015, pp. 72.

therapy. She was instructed to perform an exercise called *spider-walking*. She was directed to "walk" her fingers up a wall three times a day. Her goal was to eventually be able to raise her hand higher than her head.

She had the faith and the determination that she would soon be able to lift her arm above her head. She spider-walked up the wall, marking her progress and achievement each day. At first, she could barely lift her arm as she stretched and extended her fingers as high as she could. Sometimes her progress was no more than an eighth of an inch. But she celebrated each improvement. It took several months of exercising before she was finally able to lift her arm up over her head. Now, two years later, she can lift, turn and move her arm in any direction without even thinking about it.

On her first attempt however, she just wasn't prepared to raise her arm to its normal height. Raising her arm over her head was simply beyond her capabilities. But each morning she prepared to do a little better than she had done the night before. Little by little, a spider-step at a time, she climbed the wall and met her ultimate goal.

Spiritual preparation can happen in small steps, too. Little by little, as we add to our spiritual sustainability in the present, we develop spiritual strength for our future as well. As we increase our spiritual sustainability it will no longer matter to us if our future holds raging storms or sunlit paths, we will be prepared and need not fear.

So just what should our sustainable spirituality goals consist of? The beauty of the gospel of Jesus Christ is its simplicity. Because of its simplicity we often look passed the mark and attempt to make things more complicated than they need be. The following are a few simple goals and guidelines that will assist you in developing your spiritual strength and sustainability.

1. *Fortify your family.* Shelter your children from the onslaught of conceit, selfishness and vanity.

Secure your home against the assault of obscene and lewd cries of the world.

2. *Cultivate divine characteristics.* When we have come to "the rich knowledge of God and of Jesus our Lord" and have been given all things "necessary for life and godliness," Peter asks us to realize the potential of our divine nature by giving all diligence to the development of faith, excellence, knowledge, self-control, perseverance, godliness, brotherly kindness, and unselfish love. If you will do this, your knowledge of Christ will be full and fruitful and you will not be "nearsighted" and you "will never stumble into sin." [14] Remember that who we are is far more important than what may happen to us.

3. *Focus on Christ.* Allow your true eternal purpose to guide and direct your important life decisions. Don't become diverted by the storms and the gales you encounter on life's voyage but remember why you are here and whom you serve.

---

[14] See 2 Peter 1:2-10.

4. *Put God first.* At times you may have to make choices not based on good and evil (which is easy) but based on good and a little bit better good (which is much harder). Your safest and most secure choices will be made when you seek first the kingdom of God and its righteousness. [15]

5. *Build an earthly existence on rock,* not on sand. Wealth and material goods alone will never be able to protect you from peril and uncertainty nor will it provide lasting pleasure. However, neglecting the material necessities of life could subject you to any change in the fickle winds of fortune and lessen your potential to pursue worthy goals.

Your capacity to effectively influence and regulate the stresses of daily living is significantly affected by how you handle your physical self, circumstances and situations. Appropriately care for and respect your physical body as a designated temple for the Holy Spirit. [16] Improve your education

---

[15] See Matthew 6:33.
[16] See 1 Corinthians 3:16.

and communication skills and develop specific work habits that will allow you to successfully navigate an ever-changing economy.

Excellent physical health, suitable education, sensible money management, adequate emergency supplies and smart living are essential to a safe and secure life. They will also preserve you against the inevitable instabilities and variables of an unforeseen future. A wise nation prepares for war in peacetime. A wise person prepares for disaster in times of prosperity.

6. *Don't judge others.* The responsibility of judging people and their situations does not rest on your shoulders. Jesus tells us, "Do not judge so that you will not be judged." [17] He took it a step further when he counseled us to attend to fixing our own faults and defects before we attempt to correct and criticize others: "First remove the beam from your

---

[17] Matthew 7:1 (NET).

own eye, and then you will see clearly to remove the speck from your brother's eye." [18]

7. *Forgive.* When you forgive others and let go of grudges, criticisms and hurt feelings, you reduce the amount of stress, irritation and aggravation that deprive you of peace. Remember, you are most like Jesus Christ when you forgive the wrongs of another person.

8. *Be proactive and positive.* Do whatever you can, whatever it takes, to build your spiritual sustainability and then, in full faith, confidence and assurance, expect to see the salvation of God and his hand directing your life.

Personal and Individual Spirituality

Besides being gradual and incremental, a single step at a time, sustainable spiritual strength is personal. It's individual. What strengthens and develops your spirituality may not be the same as

---

[18] Matthew 7:5 (NET).

what strengthens and develops mine or anyone else's for that matter.

Spirituality is not part of the church we go to or the Bible study group we read with. A church can provide increased opportunities for us to improve our understanding, increase our faith and strengthen our spirituality, but no church can make us more spiritually sustainable if we don't act on the opportunities that God provides for us.

There are a lot of "Thou shalts" and "Thou shalt nots" in Christianity. We are constantly being instructed in what we "should" be doing and how we "ought" to be living.

You should read the Bible every day.

You ought to go to church every Sunday.

You need to pray every morning when you wake up and every night before you go to bed.

You should contribute to your church's relief fund, mission fund, or whatever other fund it comes up with.

Do any of those "shoulds" sound familiar to you? If so, you are not alone. But I have another "should" for you.

You should do what works best for you.

Sometimes we just have to ask ourselves what is best for us. What do we really need or want at this moment? Our spiritual growth and progression is better developed when we are moved in directions that coincide with the path our hearts and minds are following at the time. When we recognize an unsatisfied need within ourselves and work to satisfy that need in honorable activity, we enhance our possibility for spiritual improvement.

So maybe you need the practice of reading the Bible every day for an hour or so. Or perhaps you would benefit more from a close social interaction with other Christians. Or maybe your spiritual growth would be better served by witnessing to non-believers. The point is, consulting your own needs and wants at the moment, and acting on those desires, will increase your spiritual development more than following others' expectations of what you need.

So instead of listening to all the "shoulds" and "oughts" that assail our ears, perhaps we could come up with a clearer understanding of what our needs are by making more meaningful mental statements.

Rather than thinking, "I ought to go to church today," ask yourself, "How could regular, frequent church attendance add to my personal spiritual sustainability?"

As an alternative to "I should participate in the church's relief efforts" ask, "What kind of service would I enjoy doing?"

Instead of thinking, "I need to read the Bible more," ask yourself, "What has brought me the greatest joy from my scripture studies and is there a way to improve that practice?"

Instead of telling yourself you had better say a prayer tonight, consider asking yourself, "What kind of a personal communication do I have with

God? How can I improve my communication skills so that my sincere prayers will be heard and answered and I will feel the influence of his Holy Spirit?"

Do you ever wonder if the Holy Spirit is interested in what's going on in your meager, little life? When you're walking to the bus stop, or having lunch with a co-worker; when you're tending to your children or cleaning out the basement, do you feel that the Holy Spirit cares and is involved? Sometimes we may feel that the Holy Spirit only shows up for church services and then sneaks off to a distant, hidden corner of the universe for the rest of the week. That is simply not true.

Most of our lives we live outside of church, in the daily Monday through Saturday grind. But the Holy Spirit is promised to us always. If we're not feeling the influence of the Holy Spirit more often, maybe it is because we're the ones who walk out of church with a "See you next Sunday!" attitude.

Remember that spiritual development is individual. Find what works best for you as you build sustainable spiritual strength. God doesn't have just one mansion but "many mansions" and he doesn't expect us all to acquire spiritual sustainability and strength in the same exact ways. Find the things that work best for you then develop those gifts.

Being a good Christian is a full-time job all by itself. We make attempts. Sometimes we succeed but sometimes we fail. We let ourselves down and we let the Lord down. But we improve. We progress. We act a little kinder towards others. We judge a little less and we forgive a little more often. We certainly don't need to harangue ourselves for not living up to every Christian responsibility. Just as with spider-walking up a wall, progression and improvement that occur within us by a mere eighth of an inch is still progression and improvement.

Even though we tend to think in absolutes, life is not always black and white. Our time on earth is better defined as a continuum. We can look at our accomplishments and focus on the areas in life where we are making improvements. We can then let go of the missed service we could have done for an elderly neighbor, or the forgotten prayer for a sick friend that was left unsaid.

We can't do it all. What we can do is honor God by giving what time we have, utilizing what strength he has given us, from whatever position of spiritual sustainability we find ourselves at the moment. Jesus will take whatever we have to offer, no matter how little or insignificant, and he will make up the difference. That is the grace of God.

Every day we can develop our spiritual sustainability in little ways. Every morning we can reach an eighth of an inch higher than we did the night before. Listen to the needs of your own heart and spirit; then nourish them with what they most need to grow, strengthen and develop. Most of all, remember that you do not need to be troubled in your heart. Jesus has prepared the way and assures us that we will know the way as we walk it.

Two Dutch sisters, Betsie and Corrie Ten Boom, were imprisoned in Ravensbruck during World War II for sheltering Jews in their home. After their liberation, Corrie wrote this poignant vignette:

"Whenever large numbers of our Dutch women were sent away on transports, they were replaced by Polish women. These women had suffered a great deal and looked worn and anxious. We could not understand each other's language. Yet we suffered the same affliction side by side. The same Saviour had borne their griefs also.

"It was evening. A little woman was leaning wearily against the edge of her bed. She looked deeply unhappy. Betsie went to her, took her hand in her own, and said questioningly, "Jesoes Christoes?"

"A glow of happiness came over the face of the little woman. She drew Betsie to her and kissed her. The Name that is above every name united not only heaven and earth, but also the hearts of people of different tongues. These Polish Catholic women had such great love for their Saviour that the sound of His spoken name made their faces shine.

"We sometimes sang, 'Come to the Saviour, make no delay,' and they would sing it with us. The melody of that song had been imported from Poland by the Salvation Army. What the words were in Polish, I did not know. Someday we shall sing that song before the throne of God, and there will be no difference of language to separate us." [19]

As one writer has stated, "He is waiting for us to come to the mansion that he has prepared for us. He is the great measure of reality, against which other measures crumble. When his light burns in our hearts, no darkness can smother it. When he is beside us, no enemy can threaten us." [20]

Our spiritual strength and sustainability is in Jesus. Maybe we will never see the sever hardships in our lives that will test and strain our faith. But

---

[19] Corrie Ten Boom, *A Prisoner and Yet . . .* New York: Jove Publications, 1977, pp. 131-32.
[20] Author and source unknown.

every day we can rejoice in today's blessings, prepare for tomorrow's uncertainties, and develop our spiritual sustainability and faith in the Lord and Savior who died for us, who lives in us, and who also lives in anticipation of meeting us in the mansions he has prepared for us in the Kingdom of his Father.

CHAPTER THREE

ACHIEVING WORLD PEACE

World peace, or the concept of freedom, peace, and happiness within and between all nations and people, embraces the ideal of worldwide non-violence through a system of restraint that would prevent warfare. World peace refers to an end of all aggression and hostility between all humanity.

Since 1945, the United Nations (including the UK, China, Russia, France, and the US which make up the 5 permanent members of the Security Council) have struggled to settle conflicts without nations resorting to war. Nevertheless, countries have continued to engage in numerous military conflicts since that time.

Where Is Peace?

On the campus of a large university several years ago, a group of students demonstrated by waving large signs that read: "We demand peace." We live in troubled times. The majority of the world's population today is tormented by war, terrorism and unrest. Conflict exists between nations regardless of our strong desire for world peace. Politicians continually babble about sustainable and enduring peace despite our history of virtually nonstop warfare and political turmoil.

Proponents of world peace have presented a variety of theories for the achievement of global harmony and peace. I have briefly listed a few of the most popular theories.

Theories for World Peace

Imperial Peace

The Imperial Peace Theory is the oldest known theory for achieving world peace. A universal conquest wherein one nation conquers all other nations would then result is a system-wide peace. The Bronze Age of Egypt, ancient Rome, medieval China and the Inca nation are classic examples. Imperial peace is viewed as detrimental, deplorable and unachievable. Empires will inevitably fall and none possess the necessary resources to maintain even brief worldwide supremacy.

Democratic Peace

Supporters of the precarious Democratic Peace Theory allege that there is strong practical proof that democracies rarely wage war against each other. History, however, shows that several wars actually have taken place between democracies.

Capitalist Peace

Ayn Rand, in her essay, "The Roots of War," believed that capitalism created the longest period of peace in history, from the end of the Napoleonic wars in 1815 to the outbreak of World War I in 1914. The Capitalism Peace Theory suggests that most of the major wars were perpetrated by the controlled economies against the freer ones.

Cobdenism

Advocates of Cobdenism maintain that free trade precludes a nation from becoming too self-sufficient (a requisite for extended conflict) and that international free trade would render war impossible. Removing tariffs and creating free trade would make war too costly for international businesses with production, research, and sales in many different nations resulting in a powerful lobby opposed to international conflict.

Mutually Assured Destruction

The Mutually Assured Destruction Theory believes that a full-scale nuclear war between two opposing nations would essentially bring about the destruction of both aggressors. In other words, the lethality of war reaches a point where it no longer presents an advantage for either side, thereby making war pointless.

The United Nations Charter

The United Nations Charter set out after World War II to "save successive generations from the two scourges of war which twice in our lifetime has brought untold sorrow to mankind." The Charter emphasizes the acceptance of fundamental human rights, respect for international law and a unity of independent countries to preserve world peace. The Charter recognizes "the inherent dignity and...the equal and inalienable rights of all members of the human family" as the foundation of freedom, justice and "peace in the world."

Globalization

A trend has emerged in national politics wherein city-states and nation-states have united and indications suggest that the international arena will ultimately follow suit. Nations like China, Italy, the United States, Australia, Germany, India and Britain have combined into single nation-states with an implication that continued globalization will create a world-state.

Isolationism

The idea of Isolationism asserts that many nations can co-exist in peace if they have each generated a firmer focus on their own internal affairs without attempting to levy restraint on other countries. Isolationism recommends not meddling into other nations' internal affairs while emphasizing protectionism and restriction of international trade and travel.

Non-Interventionism

Non-Interventionism encourages combining free trade (like Cobdenism) with political and military non-interference. Non-Interventionism should not be confused with Isolationism.

Self-Organized Peace

Proponents of Self-Organized Peace view world peace as the result of self-determined communal activities that prevent the institutionalization of power with its subsequent aggression and hostility. World peace is seen as the outcome of a self-organized system of collectively compassionate procedures creating a sustainable politico-economic social fabric and not as the result of an investment in some political or spiritual supreme authority.

Global Union of Scientists for Peace

The Global Union of Scientists for Peace is a coalition of prominent scientists and specialists established to prevent war, terrorism and nuclear proliferation and to support safe, proven technologies for world peace. Controlling societal hostility through similar practices by small alliances has been confirmed and established throughout the world. The proven outcome shows a noticeable decrease in war, terrorism and communal aggression.

World Peace in Progress

The on-line World Peace in Progress project is designed to persuade the wealthiest, most intelligent and most powerful people in the world to employ their assets in eliminating world-wide brutality and bloodshed. Its initiators regard liberty and free enterprise as a means of achieving world peace. Their World Peace Political Center brings together approximately 3,000 of the most powerful people on earth who want to create a legacy of world peace.

Religious Views on World Peace

World religions often advocate for world peace, and each, in its own way, conveys a sincere desire to bring an end to global violence.

Bahá'í Faith

The focal objective of the Bahá'í Faith is establishing unity among the citizens of the world. Its founder, Bahá'u'lláh, affirms that "the fundamental purpose animating the Faith of God and His Religion is to safeguard the interests and promote the unity of the human race." The eventual end goal of the Bahá'í Faith is seen as a time of spiritual and social unity where all of humanity candidly connects with and cares for one another, instead of merely tolerating each other.

Buddhism

Buddhists consider anger (and other negative states of mind) as the root causes of war and fighting and that world peace will only be attained if we first establish peace within our minds. Buddhists believe people can live in peace and harmony by abandoning negative thoughts and emotions and by fostering positive emotions such as love and compassion.

Buddhists have been integral to the movement toward world peace and have built Peace Pagodas to symbolize and inspire humanity to pursue world peace.

Hinduism

The essence of the ancient Hindu concept of Vasudha eka kutumbakam (the world is one family) is the belief that only corrupt minds see disharmony and opposition. Through greater wisdom we become more inclusive and free ourselves from worldly illusions. World peace can only be achieved through the internal process of liberating ourselves from the man-made boundaries that separate the human race.

Jainism

A central concept of Jainism is compassion for all life, whether human or non-human. Human life is seen as a rare and exceptional opportunity to gain enlightenment. Killing anyone for any reason is considered unthinkable and abhorrent. Jainism requires all participants to be vegetarian. Jainism's view on World Peace is captured in the words of Virchand Gandhi: "May peace rule the universe; may peace rule in kingdoms and empires; may peace rule in states and in the lands of the potentates; may peace rule in the house of friends and may peace also rule in the house of enemies."

Sikhism

Peace comes from God and there can be no worship without the performance of good deeds. Guru Nanak stressed that a Sikh should balance vocation, veneration, and charity, and defend the rights of all creatures. They are persuaded to live with optimistic resilience and a concept of sharing, giving charitable donations, and working for the good of the community and others.

Non-violence is a central concept of all Dharmic religions (Hinduism, Jainism, Buddhism and Sikhism).

Islam

Inner peace for Islam involves unequivocal faith and obedience to the only one God who is the source of Ultimate Peace. A common ancestry commencing with Adam and Eve serves as a reminder to quell the lethal ideology of ethnic superiority and enables people to live collectively on a common planet in peace and harmony.

"O mankind, we created you from a male and female, and rendered you distinct peoples and tribes, that you may recognize and know one another. The best among you in the sight of God is the most righteous. Certainly, God is Omniscient, All-Aware."[21]

Knowing God brings true peace to the soul. When we have obtained peace within, we can then develop truly peaceful relationships with others. Islam awaits the second coming of the prophet Isa (Jesus) when love and peace will make this world resemble paradise.

Judaism

World peace or the notion of "repairing the world" (Tikkun olam) is a fundamental principle of Judaism. Tikkun olam is accomplished through

---

21 Qur'an 49:13.

compassion and integrity, through obedience to God's law, and through persuading others to behave morally. Jewish tradition awaits a future Messiah or "king appointed by God" to return the Jews to Israel, after which the world will experience unending worldwide peace and prosperity.

"And he shall judge between the nations and reprove many peoples, and they shall beat their swords into plowshares and their spears into pruning hooks; nation shall not lift the sword against nation, neither shall they learn war anymore." [22]

Christianity

Christian belief indicates that any semblance of world peace will only be achieved through the Word of God and by the love of God as exemplified in the life of Jesus Christ. Obtaining peace requires good works and forgiveness toward those who do wrong. A distinct difference in Christianity, however,

---

[22] Yeshayahu 2:4.

is that Christians do not expect to achieve worldwide peace until that peace is established upon the "new Earth" foretold in Revelation 21.

The Book of Matthew quotes Christ as saying: "Do not suppose that I have come to bring peace to the earth. I did not come to bring peace, but a sword. For I have come to turn a man against his father, a daughter against her mother, a daughter-in-law against her mother-in-law—a man's enemies will be the members of his own household." [23]

With such an ominous prospect looming in our lives, how do we find peace in our world? How to we achieve peace in the presence of fear? The ideology of man and the ways of the world will certainly continue to deliver chaos and confusion.

James addressed the cause of war and world conflict in a letter he wrote to Israel: "Where do wars and fightings among you come from? Don't they

---

[23] Matthew 10:34-36 (NET).

come from your pleasures that war in your members. You lust, and don't have. You kill, covet, and can't obtain. You fight and make war. Yet you don't have, because you don't ask. You ask, and don't receive, because you ask amiss, so that you may spent it for your pleasures." [24]

At the time James wrote this, the Jews were in open rebellion against Rome. They were fighting to preserve their religion and to procure their freedom. They had become divided into splinter groups and were fighting among themselves all the while they waged war against Egypt, Syria, and others. They were both slaughtering and being slaughtered. And so James posed the question, Doesn't war and fighting stem from your pursuit of pleasure, your passions and your lust? [25]

The Jewish conflicts and aggressions were bred from their lust which is the very same incentive

---

[24] James 4:1-3 (WEB).
[25] See James 4:1.

for the wars that continue to distress and torment our world today. History is a repetitious recital of deliberate and dissolute destruction of human life and personal property. A country covets another country's territory or property and forces its way of life on them through physical violence. Each nation will massacre, devastate, and demolish until one is overpowered. All the while the politicians promise and the people pray for world peace.

Peace has very different and distinct meanings and interpretations. The Greek word for peace denotes an end to or an absence from aggression between conflicting factions. It is simply the opposite of war and contention. The Hebrew word for peace, however, is far more comprehensive in meaning.

It has been commonly used as a greeting, "Peace be with you."

It also defines domestic peace between husband and wife and harmonious relations within families and among friends.

It also denotes peace of mind or serenity inspired by a proper relationship with God.

Due to these distinct definitions, our search for peace will lead us in very different directions. The condition of world peace that society is seeking represents an end to international hostilities and violence. But sustainable world peace is achievable only within the conditions established by God.

Isaiah explained that: "You will keep him in perfect peace, whose mind is stayed on you; because he trusts in you." [26] This perfect peace is achievable only through a belief in God. Inner peace and tranquility can be found in following correct gospel principles founded in Jesus Christ's teachings. Inner peace would then become familial peace, then

---

[26] Isaiah 26:3 (WEB).

communal peace, then national peace and even world peace. But an unbelieving world would never be able to reconcile such an idea.

Peace in the Presence of Fear

It is a knowledge and understanding of spiritual matters that makes the difference in whether Christians view the future with anxiety or with anticipation—with fear or with hope. The strength of our souls, not the circumstances of our lives, chases away the fear in our hearts and assures the establishment of peace within. With a "perfect love" that "drives out fear," [27] Jesus consistently and persistently declares the way of peace in the midst of suffering and turmoil, present or future, expected or unexpected. Whether for individuals or for families, for communities or for churches, there are two critical ways in which we can become more spiritually strengthened to better sustain our faith in troubling and turbulent times and to experience the

---

[27] 1 John 4:18 (NET).

peace that Jesus has promised us. One way is to prepare for what is ahead and the other way is to build on a sure and unshakeable foundation.

Preparation:

Our individual sustainability in the face of the coming challenges and difficulties depends less on the nature of those tumultuous circumstances or events and more on our own spiritual power to respond positively and effectively. We can view the predicted events of the future in terms of current trends, uncertain contingencies, or our own spiritual purposes.

When we look at the future from the vantage point of current trends, we frequently see the future as an extension of the present. But we cannot, of course, accurately determine what influences and activities will remain after today and continue to be influential into the future.

When we consider contingencies—possible but uncertain circumstances, such as, earthquakes, tsunamis, fires, wars, and economic recessions or, on the opposite side, greater education and improved opportunities for work—the challenge becomes preparing ourselves to minimize the worst and accentuate the best depending on which events actually transpire.

When we see the future in terms of our spiritual purposes, we attempt to design attitudes and ambitions that will shape our future and positively influence our choices. The challenge becomes properly identifying the attitudes that will survive troublesome times and challenging circumstances and establishing for ourselves worthwhile objectives and ambitions.

Whichever method we use to envision the future, our real purpose is to develop faith and confidence in the face of uncertainty and fear. We cannot predict the future, but we can prepare for it. Our faith and confidence will increase as we begin taking practical steps to lessen life's hazards and strengthen our own determination during difficult conditions.

Maintaining peace in the present and sustainable spiritual strength in the future is found in who we are, what we capable of doing, and what we have done to minimize our risk. It is found in the strength of our principles and the grandeur of our goals. We should not merely wait for future events to unfold; we should think, work, and prepare to deal with them.

A Sure and Unshakeable Foundation:

Faith is a necessary part of our lives. Doubt and faith cannot exist in the same person at the same time. If we harbor doubts and fear, we will not have unshakeable confidence and our faith will become ineffectual and unsustainable. If our faith is weak it will not sustain us spiritually against the opposition, tribulation, and affliction which we will encounter as Christians.

The French philosopher and mathematician Blaise Pascal wrote: "There is a virtuous fear which is the effect of faith and a vicious fear which is the product of doubt and distrust. The former leads to hope as relying on God in whom we believe; the latter inclines to despair, as not relying upon God, in whom we do not believe. Persons of one character fear to lose God; those of the other character fear to find him." [28]

Two forces are battling to win our souls. Two opposing powers grapple continuously to gain our devotion. John foresaw the day when the just will come together in a deadly conflict, at Armageddon, against the forces of evil. These evil forces are busy preparing for that battle. They are arrayed against us but we are not alone in our struggle. We have been promised help, aid, and assistance in achieving victory in the war against evil.

---

[28] Blaise Pascal (1623–62), in Tyron Edwards, *The New Dictionary of Thoughts*, p. 196.

We are dual creatures with both a spiritual nature and a physical body. Just as light radiates from the sun and fills the solar system, there is a power and spirit and an influence radiating from God that fills the immensity of space. The influence that comes from God, comes to us through our spiritual nature, not through the physical body. His help and support affect us through the spiritual senses and by spiritual power. The power emanating from God is just as real as the light of the sun, and just as the physical body is sensitive to sunlight, our spiritual nature is sensitive and sensible to the light and power of God.

Job explains to us that, "There is a spirit in man; and the inspiration of the Almighty giveth them understanding." [29] We are not merely physical beings; we are spiritual beings as well. Our knowledge of the meaning of life and our unique view of faith is displayed in Jesus' warning to his apostles: "Do not be afraid of those who kill the body

---

[29] Job 32:8 (KJV).

but cannot kill the soul. Instead, fear the one who is able to destroy both soul and body in hell." [30]

People who are spiritually asleep are in a sorrowful and unsustainable situation. They have no refuge, no promise of help, no power and no strength to fight the forces of evil that seek our destruction. People cannot safely walk through the ups and downs and the dangers of life without the help of the Lord. This is why he pleads with us to constantly seek him.

King David declared: "If I ascend up into heaven, you are there. If I make my bed in Sheol, behold, you are there!" [31] By the presence and power of his Spirit, God is everywhere. In the midst of the trials and turmoil that surround us, we need to turn to this source of strength to sustain us and support us to weather the approaching storms of life. There is an abundance of power available to everyone who

---

[30] Matthew 10:28 (NET).
[31] Psalms 139:8 (WEB).

sincerely and honestly seeks to make themselves strong enough to succeed and attain victory over the devil and all his schemes against the human soul. Herein rests the efficacy of Christ's instruction to "be not troubled." [32]

The promise of peace is extended only to those who believe in God and obey his law and commandments. Isaiah described the decadence and depravity of certain leaders, then added: "The wicked are like the troubled sea; for it can't rest, and its waters cast up mire and dirt. There is no peace, says my God, to the wicked." [33]

The wicked receive no peace, and their unrighteous activities cheat the rest of us out of our promise of peace. World conflicts are usually instigated by a small but powerful minority who thoughtlessly and ruthlessly bring suffering and sorrow to millions of innocent people.

---

[32] Matthew 24:6 (KJV).
[33] Isaiah 57: 20, 21 (WEB).

The innocent victims of oppressors have always prayed for peace. They have demonstrated and rioted and even died in an effort to bring an end to violence and hostility. Sustainable world peace will be achieved only through the means that Jesus gave peace to his disciples and "not as the world does." [34]

Emerson wrote, "Nothing can bring you peace but yourself; nothing can bring you peace but the triumph of principles." [35] The principles that will ultimately bring peace are found in the gospel of Jesus Christ. Rejecting Christ and his teachings creates insecurity, inner-conflict, and contention. Peace comes through absolute submission to the Prince of peace.

When we accept Jesus, we will find peace. Jesus taught us that in the world we would have trouble and suffering, [36] but that we could find peace

---

[34] John 14:27 (NET).
[35] Source Unknown.
[36] See John 16:33.

in a world of conflict if we accept his great gift and invitation: "Come to me, all you who are weary and burdened, and I will give you rest. Take my yoke on you, and learn from me, because I am gentle and humble in heart, and you will find rest for your souls." [37]

A great writer named Fenelon said, "Peace does not dwell in outward things, but within the soul; we may preserve it in the midst of the bitterest pain, if our will remains firm and submissive. Peace in this life springs from acquiescence, not in an exemption from suffering." [38]

This peace protects us from a world in conflict. Knowing that God lives and loves us pacifies the troubled heart. The key to achieving sustainable world peace is faith in God and in his Son, Jesus Christ. Only this will bring us lasting peace.

---

[37] Matthew 11:28, 29 (NET).
[38] Source Unknown.

Faith in Jesus is the foundation of peace in this life and the greatest defense against fear, hopelessness and depression. Just before Jesus took on the suffering of Gethsemane and Golgotha he blessed his apostles: "Peace I leave with you, my peace I give to you: I do not give it as the world does. Do not let your hearts be distressed or lacking in courage." [39] With unshakeable faith built upon the foundation of Christ, we, too, can know this peace, and can also witness with Paul that "God did not give us a Spirit of fear but of power and love and self-control." [40]

---

[39] John 14:27 (NET).
[40] 2 Timothy 1:7 (NET).

CHAPTER FOUR

THE REAL OIL CRISIS

When a youth group from a local church was asked what one question they would most like to ask Jesus about his second coming, three particular questions came up over and over. As we might expect, "When will it happen?" was the most-asked question. The second question varied in wording but contained essentially a similar idea: "What will life be like before he comes?" Not surprisingly, the third most frequently asked question was, "What can I do to be ready?" We would probably all love to know the answers to the first two questions, but the answer to the third question seems significantly more pressing and important.

The second coming of Jesus Christ is portrayed by Malachi in his paradoxical phrase "the great and terrible day of the Lord." [41] We must wonder how a day could possibly be both great and terrible simultaneously. The future shoulders some outrageous and appalling events—wars, murders, wickedness, violent storms, great earthquakes, floods, food shortages, sickness and disease. Alternatively, the future will also convey many events that make it a great day—the Kingdom of God will devour all other kingdoms, [42] and Jesus will return to separate the wheat from the weeds. [43]

So just what determines whether it's a great day or a terrible day for us individually? How does the faithful Christian look toward an uncertain future with faith and anxious anticipation instead of

---

[41] Malachi 4:5 (NET).
[42] See Daniel 2:44.
[43] See Matthew 13:30.

with fear and apprehension? Whether we see Jesus' return as a great day or a terrible day depends largely on how sustainable our faith and spirituality are today. If we want to be ready for what the future holds, we need to strengthen our faith in Jesus Christ.

After encouraging his disciples to not be alarmed, the Lord mentioned a proverb that was common in the Holy Land at that time: "Learn this parable from the fig tree: Whenever its branch becomes tender and puts out its leaves, you know that summer is near." [44]

Since the fig tree is one of the last trees to put forth leaves, it became common in the Middle East to say that if there were leaves starting on the fig tree then summer had arrived and the cold weather was over. Jesus compared the leaves of the fig tree to the signs of the times: "So also you, when you see these things happening, know that he is near, right at the

---

[44] Mark 13:28 (NET).

door...Watch out! Stay alert! For you do not know when the time will come." [45] Jesus has counseled us to watch for the signs of the times. Like the leaves of the fig tree, certain specific signs will indicate that his coming is near.

Much of what the future holds may not be pleasant. Some of what awaits the world because of its wickedness is dreadful and deeply depressing. But God has given us a knowledge of the future—even of the terrible events—so that when they occur we will recognize them as the fulfillment of God's word. We will see them as proof that his word is all being fulfilled.

The parable of the ten virgins evokes a brilliant portrayal of a Middle Eastern wedding. George Mackie, a Christian minister who lived much of his life in the Holy Land, described a Palestinian

---

[45] Mark 13: 29, 33 (NET).

wedding ceremony with the following rich and revealing imagery:

"Oriental marriages," he wrote, "usually take place in the evening.... The whole attention is turned to the public arrival of the bridegroom to receive the bride prepared for him and waiting in the house among her female attendants....

"As the hours drag on their topics of conversation become exhausted, and some of them grow tired and fall asleep. There is nothing more to be done, and everything is in readiness for the reception of the bridegroom, when the cry is heard outside announcing his approach.

"The bridegroom meanwhile is absent, spending the day at the house of one of his relatives. There, soon after sunset, that is between seven and eight o'clock, his male friends begin to assemble.... The time is occupied with light refreshments, general conversation and the recitation of poetry in praise of the two families chiefly concerned and of the bridegroom in particular. After all have been courteously welcomed and their congratulations received, the bridegroom, about eleven o'clock, intimates his wish to set out. Flaming torches are then held aloft by special bearers, lit candles are handed at the door to each visitor as he goes out, and the procession sweeps slowly along toward the house where the bride and her female attendants are waiting. A great crowd has meanwhile assembled on the balconies, garden-walls, and flat roofs of the houses on each side of the road.... The bridegroom is the centre of interest. Voices are heard whispering, 'There he is! There he is!' From time to time women raise their voices in the peculiar shrill, wavering shriek by which joy is expressed at marriages and other times of family and public rejoicing. The sound is heard at a great distance, and is repeated by other voices in advance of the procession, and thus intimation is given of the approach half an hour or more before the marriage escort arrives.... As the house is approached the excitement increases, the bridegroom's pace is quickened, and the alarm is raised in louder tones and more repeatedly, 'He is coming, he is coming!'

"Before he arrives, the maidens in waiting come forth with lamps and candles a short distance to light up the entrance, and do honour to the bridegroom and the group of relatives and intimate friends around him. These pass into the final rejoicing and the marriage supper; the others who have discharged their duty in accompanying him to the door, immediately disperse, and the door is shut." [46]

In Jesus' day and time, olive oil was used to fuel the small clay or brass lamps people carried outside at night to light their steps. Outfitted with a short wick, the lamps were small enough to fit in the palm of a hand and obviously held only a minimal amount of oil. They could burn for about an hour

---

[46] George Mackie, *Bible Manners and Customs* (New York: Fleming H. Revell, 1898), 123-26.

before going out. It seems to me that the olive oil is the principle part of this parable.

So just what does the olive oil represent? The olive oil is a representation of the Holy Spirit whose influence is often portrayed as burning and fire. The Bible speaks of being baptized with "the Holy Spirit and with fire." [47] The Spirit of God is a source of light and truth and the olive oil, as far as the parable is concerned at least, denotes the light and power of the Holy Spirit.

The ten virgins represent the followers of Christ and not the general population of the world. All ten of them, both the wise and the foolish, had accepted the invitation to the wedding supper. They were not pagans or heathens. They were the ones who had been invited to participate in that all-important symbolic event. But half of them were

---

[47] Matthew 3:11 (NET).

foolishly unprepared for the important event that would affect their future.

Consider how the five wise virgins were different from the five foolish ones. All of them were virgins and all of them had brought their lamps. The only difference was the extra supply of olive oil the wise virgins had brought with them. When we recognize the imagery employed in this parable, then the message becomes obvious. All of us need to have an extra portion of the Holy Spirit if we expect to be prepared for Christ's coming. Jesus has given us this parable as a special warning.

It is in the darkest hours of our lives that heaven offers joy in exchange for our weariness. In the daylight hours it is often difficult to distinguish between the wise and the foolish but the midnight shadows will reveal our wisdom. Precisely at the darkest hour Christ will come and there will be no more time to prepare. The foolish virgins wanted the wise to share the oil they had brought with them but sustainable spirituality cannot simply be handed to us. Faith, obedience and a knowledge of God cannot simply be given away. Each of us must obtain for ourselves the necessary oil to provide us with enough light to endure the darkness.

In the parable, olive oil could be purchased at the market. In real life, spiritual oil is collected one drop at a time through Christ-like living. Church attendance, prayer, witnessing to others, studying God's word and every act of devotion adds a drop of oil to our lamps. Righteous thoughts and acts of kindness add to the supply of oil we can use at midnight to refuel our dimming lamps.

Seeing how imperative it is to have the Holy Spirit with us in troubling times, the real oil crisis of our time is not the one that we see at the gas pumps. The single greatest factor to sustainable spirituality is to live so that we can have the influence and guidance of the Holy Spirit to witness to us of Christ's truth and to help us avoid deception. The parable of the ten virgins teaches us how to become spiritually sustainable by living so that we will have the influence of the Holy Spirit to give us testimony and guide us through the darkness ahead.

The Holy Spirit is our close companion when we live the gospel of Christ. Obeying Jesus' teachings is the only way to ensure that our lamps are filled with oil. Christ has given each one of us a lamp. Whether or not there is any oil in our lamp is up to us. If we follow Jesus' teachings and example, we will have an adequate supply of the necessary oil to light our way through the darkness. We cannot borrow from others. We can only purchase oil from the eternal supply offered at the fountain of truth, our Savoir, Jesus Christ. Whether or not we have oil in our lamps is solely determined by our individual faithfulness to him.

CHAPTER FIVE

ENDING WORLD HUNGER

We live in times of uncertainty. More people are unemployed in the United States than have been since the Great Depression. The number of families suffering hunger and privation has reached levels not seen since Lyndon Johnson declared a war on poverty in the 1960s. Nations are divided politically, economically, and socially. In the near term, the prospects for ending world hunger seem dim, at best.

One enormous stumbling block to achieving a sustainable world environment is the alleviation of starvation and poverty. According to the Brundtland Commission report, *Our Common Future*, poverty is a source of environmental degradation. The report indicates that "poverty is a major cause and effect of global environmental problems. It is therefore futile to attempt to deal with environmental problems without a broader perspective that encompasses the factors underlying world poverty and international inequality." [48] Populations existing in poverty rely heavily on local ecosystems as a resource for fundamental needs such as nutrition, medicine and general well-being.

The grim and horrifying pictures of starving humanity in India, Africa and many other nations throughout the world reveal the scrawny limbs, the bloated stomachs, and the undernourished faces of these poor, unfortunate masses suffering from the lack of adequate food to nourish and build up their bodies.

---

[48] The Brundtland Commission Report, *Our Common Future*.

As horrific as this deprivation is, an even ghastlier famine was predicted by the Old Testament Prophet Amos who forewarned:

"Behold, the days come, saith the Lord God, that I will send a famine in the land, not a famine of bread, nor a thirst for water, but of hearing the words of the Lord:

"And they shall wander from sea to sea, and from the north even to the east, they shall run to and fro to seek the word of the Lord, and shall not find it." [49]

The sight of millions who have starved themselves from the fully-sustaining divine food that could render them spiritually strong and wholesome with a vital and living faith is no less tragic! On the one hand, we witness the mortal homicide brought on humanity through greed and avarice; on the other we see the self-inflicted curse of spiritual suicide.

---

[49] Amos 8:11,12 (KJV).

Throughout my lifetime I have been indoctrinated to accept the claim that our world has become overpopulated. A recent United Nations International Conference on Population and Development held in Cairo, Egypt centered their debate around what they call "sustainable growth." Not many people in the developed nations of the world would argue against such a socially acceptable phrase as "sustainable growth" despite the Biblical command to "Be fruitful and multiply! Fill the earth and subdue it!" [50]

In the September 1994 issue of Forbes Magazine, a carefully thought-out editorial maintains that people are actually an asset and not a liability to our planet. It candidly pronounces as preposterous the widely accepted premise that a decrease in population growth is necessary for economic development. The editorial convincingly

---

[50] Genesis 1:28 (NET).

declares that "free people don't exhaust resources; they create them." [51]

Furthermore, a U.S. News and World Report article maintains that the Earth is able to produce food for a population of at least eighty billion! This is eight times the expected ten billion estimated to populate the planet by 2050 A.D. Another study suggests that through further developed and enhanced scientific techniques, the earth could feed as many as one thousand billion people. [52]

Those who argue for sustainable growth lack vision and faith. Spiritual sustainability comes from being rooted and grounded in the gospel of Jesus Christ. When we are settled in the faith, securely fastened to principles of truth, we will become nourished by the word of God. We do not need to starve ourselves seeking truth in the false ideas, philosophies and vagaries of a godless humanity.

---

[51] Forbes Magazine, 12 September 1994, p. 25.
[52] *Ten Billion for Dinner, Please.* U.S. News and World Report, 12 September 1994, pp. 57-60.

The Christian foundation for truth has Jesus Christ as the chief cornerstone. [53]

Every builder knows that a good building with a bad foundation is not only useless but also dangerous. John Stott explains that "If the stability of buildings depends largely on their foundations, so does the stability of human lives. The search for personal security is a primal instinct, but many fail to find it today. Old familiar landmarks are being obliterated. Moral absolutes which were once thought to be eternal are being abandoned." [54] Our house of faith is only as secure as the foundation it is built on. When human support fails us, our hearts must be riveted on the things of the Spirit, those internal realities that provide meaning, perspective, and the necessary sustenance for all that matters in life.

---

[53] See Ephesians 2:19-20.
[54] Stott, John, *Life in Christ*, p. 22.

A Jewish tradition claims that during the early stages of construction of the Jewish temple, the builders mistakenly discarded the cornerstone. Centuries later, Jesus spoke of people disregarding him and his message. "Have you never read in the scriptures; 'The stone the builders rejected has become the cornerstone. This is from the Lord, and it is marvelous in our eyes.'?" [55]

The challenge for those who aspire to Christian discipleship is to build our lives on Christ, to construct a house of faith where his Spirit can reside. There is safety only in Christ. There is security only in his word and through his infinite and eternal power. But with so many babbling voices enticing us into forbidden paths how do we know the Way, live the Truth, and gain that Life which is so abundantly offered to us?

In our overly complex world we find people eagerly selling solutions to all our troubles. People

---

[55] Matthew 21:42, (NET) compare Psalm 118:22-23, Acts 4:11.

gorge themselves on self-improvement programs, internet blogs, magazine articles, seminars, courses and workshops. They eat up the idea of self-discovery, learning who they are and what they can achieve. They eagerly devour programs that foster personal worth and self-esteem. They gobble down the philosophy that the answer to their personal problems lies deep within and that the key to understanding and correcting their attitudes and actions lies buried deep in their past. They feed on the popular teaching that their problems are a product of how people mistreated them and that they need to work through those relationships to become whole. With all of this, they are still starving for truth.

Underlying this "pursuit of excellence" is a very revealing philosophy that deep-seated problems can only be solved by professional therapists and counselors and that feasting on the word of God, studying the Bible, praying, forgiving others, repenting, and making righteous choices based on Christ's gospel are all too simplistic and inadequate in dealing with today's difficult challenges.

In his eye-opening book, *The Screwtape Letters*, C. S. Lewis portrays an archdevil named Screwtape training his nephew, Wormwood, how to deceive Christians.

"The real trouble about the set your patient is living in," explains Screwtape, "is that it is merely Christian. They all have individual interests, of course, but the bond remains mere Christianity. What we want, if men become Christians at all, is to keep them in the state of mind I call 'Christianity And.' You know—Christianity and the Crisis, Christianity and the New Psychology, Christianity and the New Order, Christianity and Faith Healing, Christianity and Psychical Research, Christianity and Vegetarianism, Christianity and Spelling Reform. If they must be Christians, let them at least be Christians with a difference. Substitute for the faith itself some Fashion with a Christian colouring. Work on their horror of the Same Old Thing." [56]

The devil doesn't really require us to lie or cheat or steal. All he needs is for us to ignore, lessen and devalue the power and significance of the teachings of Jesus Christ.

Our expanding world of information and technology creates a challenge for Christians worldwide to feast on the fundamentals and the basic, simple teachings of the gospel. New discoveries will continue to relieve human suffering and free humanity from many of life's struggles, but some things will never change. Some things are resolved only through divine intervention.

Paul taught that in Christ "all the fullness of deity lives in bodily form, and you have been filled in

---

[56] C.S. Lewis, *The Screwtape Letters*, pp. 115-116.

him, who is the head over every ruler and authority."[57]

Too often we underestimate the magnitude of the love and power of Jesus Christ in re-creating and renewing the human personality. The Spirit of God is incredibly therapeutic. The love of God extends far beyond any earthly substitute. In seeking solutions to life's problems, we should consider the word of God and the guidance of the Holy Spirit as seriously as we consider the ideas and standards of humanity.

Our preoccupation with success and excellence, to a degree, is commendable in that it helps us focus on the tasks-at-hand and assists us in being more effective. But we need perspective. I don't diminish the value of personal achievement and growth or the striving for excellence as long as part of our striving includes the deep desire to find

---

[57] Colossians 2:9-10 (NET).

God and to accept the procedures he offers to enlarge our lives and our souls.

Modern pursuits of excellence often become an attempt to please or impress other people. In the final analysis, other people are not our judge, and giving too much attention to their positive or negative judgments can actually undermine our relationship with God and our development of sound Christian values.

We should have grand goals in life and do what we can to achieve them. But our personal goals should be in harmony with God's grander purpose for us. As my wife often reminds me, "Do you want what you want, or do you want something better?"

The power of life and salvation is in Christ. His grace is sufficient to heal us if we yield and submit and rely on Him. Jesus came to change human nature. We, on the other hand, want to solve our problems in our own way. We renew or remake our personality through some personal behavior modification plan. We work on our flaws and weaknesses for extended periods then advance to another, then another.

Our efforts certainly have merit as they encourage us to eliminate our character flaws. Benjamin Franklin used just such a system for self-improvement. But sometimes it's like trying to hold a hundred ping pong balls under water at the same time. Eventually, some are going to pop up out of the water. In attempting to re-submerge those, more will find their way to the surface.

Our sins and short-comings are similar in making it impractical and even impossible to change our lives that way. If you want to get your life in order consider an alternative approach—ask God to make you a new creature in Christ, to give you a clean heart and an educated conscience.

God's way is so much more effective, so much more satisfying, and so much less frustrating. He asks us to be born again, to have our natures changed so that we will have no desire to engage in our old sinful ways. He asks us to acknowledge our weakness and human limitations and to demonstrate faith in his power to renew and refine us.

We should do our best to overcome bad habits but at the same time lean on that arm that is mighty to save. Then we will notice changes in our nature. We can strengthen our resolve with the following 3 steps:

1. *Feast on the words of the Lord.*

The scriptures contain the words of Christ. Reading and studying them is how we hear the voice of the Master. The Bible has been written and endorsed to bring us to Christ and to establish us in his doctrine. When we become serious students of the Bible, striving to understand and apply scriptural precepts and principles, we will readily see the hand of God in our lives and we can better discern the handiwork of Satan. We become better equipped to sift through the sordid and further prepared to distinguish the divine from the diabolical and the sacred from the secular.

The word of God helps us recognize and refute teachings and ideas that take us on intellectual and philosophic detours. It allows us to cut through false notions and to discard counterfeit philosophies that may seem pleasing to the human intellect but are in reality damaging to our spiritual sustainability. It allows us to become grounded and settled in truth, anchored to the Lord's word and built on the rock of Christ.

2. *Share this spiritual food.*

Spiritual power accompanies those who share the word of the Lord with people who are starving for spiritual sustenance. Human philosophy, however pleasantly stated or however admirable and appropriate it may appear, simply cannot connect with the soul in the same way the doctrines of Christ can. If we teach the gospel of Christ with the power and persuasion of the Holy Spirit, others will be turned to Christ.

3. *Trust in God.*

There is a power in Christ not only to calm the seas but also to calm the storms of the human heart, to mend the hurt of broken and defeated souls.

There is a power in Christ to assume the obligation of our sins, for we cannot remit our own sins any more than we can resurrect ourselves. We are, truly, saved by the grace of our God.

When we are contaminated by sin and enveloped in the spiritual darkness which follows transgression, it is often hard for us to see how to disentangle ourselves. And even when we are brought to see the way of life and truth, we may find it difficult to follow. The fact that we have lost virtue may evidence a weakness of character, making it hard for us to apply the principles by which we can regain innocence and acquire spiritual strength.

Nevertheless, the pangs of guilt and remorse of conscience which sinners feel may awaken in us a desire for righteousness and with a new determination to do right, coupled with the mercy and power which God extends to those who truly desire to come unto him, we can be renewed to a state of purity and power in Christ.

We must learn to trust in him more. We must learn to rely on him more. We must learn to surrender our burdens to him more. We must be willing to seek that grace or enabling power which will make up the difference, that sacred power which indeed makes all the difference!

Our challenge to discern good from evil, light from darkness, virtue from vice, includes discerning between things that matter most from those things of little or no real value. Disputatious ideas steal our time and attention. Dissonant voices absorb our interest. We should be more discriminating with our time, interest and attention. Some things simply matter more than others and the thing that matters most is the knowledge and testimony of Jesus. "For no one can lay any other foundation than what is being laid, which is Jesus Christ." [58]

God will assist us in our problems in a way quite different from the solutions offered by the world. If you thirst for excellence, the world will offer you a glass of water. You can drink it and get on with your life, your career, your family responsibilities and make your way in the world. But Jesus Christ can offer you a well of water, a spring of eternal life, and you need never thirst again. This water is essential to our spiritual sustainability.

Living Water to Quench Spiritual Thirst

Several years ago a local newspaper printed a story of a Boy Scout in Arizona who died from heat exhaustion after his water ran out. The Scout troop had not counted on three days of record-breaking temperatures in the Arizona desert. While searching

---

[58] 1 Corinthians 3:11(NET).

for water in the 112-degree heat, one Scout fainted just 100 yards from the Colorado River. He died a short time later. The unexpected loss of this young boy's life, the anguish of his fellow Scouts and the heartbreak of his sorrowing parents all contribute to make this such a distressing tragedy.

I have wondered many times since about those who are dying spiritually from a thirst for living water. Perhaps there is someone just a hundred yards from living water who is suffering spiritual exhaustion or dying of spiritual thirst.

The article in the newspaper followed the tragic account of the Boy Scout's demise with a list of survival tips for desert hikers. The same survival techniques apply to surviving the spiritual deserts we encounter in life.

1. Take adequate water with you. Drink at least a gallon of water a day and more during extremely hot weather.

How much spiritual water do we have available in a time of spiritual crisis? Can we stave off spiritual exhaustion with just a sip from a cup or do we need to drink deeply from the words of the Bible or the power of prayer when things become particularly hot?

2. Carry all your water with you. Don't depend on natural sources along the trail.

We must become spiritually self-reliant. We will all need to carry our own living water with us and we will have to be guided by the light within. If we do not carry this water ourselves, we may not survive. We must prepare ourselves spiritually for any difficult time ahead.

3. Always hike with an experienced guide, one who is familiar with the area.

As Christians we have an infallible guide. We have the Holy Spirit to direct us. We will hear this direction in our minds and in our hearts as we pray for guidance and bearing in our lives.

If we pray fervently and follow the directions of our Guide, and if we read our survival manual, the Bible, every day (and more when the temperatures are hot and temptations are strong) then this living water will quench our spiritual thirst and save our spiritual lives.

The Lord feels an unconditional love for each one of us, with all our weaknesses and imperfections, our wrong choices and mistakes. He offers us living water while we suffer a dry and parched thirst. Will we fill our buckets from the well of living water at church? Will we drink deeply from the messages of living water in the Bible or will we simply take a sip from the cup and travel on?

We must quench our spiritual thirst at the fountain of living waters and then fill our pitchers, our canteens, and our vessels and carry the living water with us through the deserts of life. And then, we should share that water with anyone along the way who is suffering spiritual thirst because they simply don't know where to find this living water.

Jehovah acknowledged ancient Israel's double sin, declaring, "My people have committed a double wrong: they have rejected me, the fountain of life-giving water, and they have dug cisterns for themselves, cracked cisterns which cannot even hold water." [59] Rejecting or ignoring God is a serious matter. We must not turn a deaf ear to his divine direction.

The Lord is the Way. When we refuse his message we step onto a broad road headed for destruction. The Lord is the Truth. When we snub his teachings we wander in ignorance. The Lord is the Light. When we forsake him we walk in darkness. The Lord is the Life. When we refuse to unite with his will we are courting spiritual death. The Lord is the Fountain of Living Waters. When we forsake him

---

[59] Jeremiah 2:13 (NET).

we stop the flow of living water that would quench the world's gasping thirst.

No relief will come to our parched and scorched souls by digging our own reservoirs. Human-made reservoirs will be insufficient and undersupplied. They cannot hold the spiritual water that would provide us delivery from the afflictions of the future.

Our supply of living water is never in question unless we shut off the flow ourselves. The Lord promises, "I will pour water upon him that is thirsty, and floods upon the dry ground: I will pour my spirit upon thy seed, and my blessing upon thine offspring." [60] The source of living water is abundant and full. We can drink all we need and still have enough to share with everyone around us.

---

[60] Isaiah 44:3 (KJV).

CHAPTER SIX

RENEWABLE ENERGY

Energy consumed at insignificant rates compared to its supply and with governable environmental effects is what we call sustainable energy. Technologies that support sustainable energy include renewable energy sources, such as hydroelectricity, solar energy, wind energy, wave power, geothermal energy, and other technologies designed to improve energy efficiency.

Climate change concerns coupled with high oil prices and increased government support are creating an enhanced interest in the sustainable energy industry. Moving toward increased sustainable energy will require changes not only in the way energy is supplied, but in the way it is used, reducing the amount of energy required to deliver various goods or services.

Energy efficiency and renewable energy are said to be the twin pillars of sustainable energy. Creating sustainable energy will require the provision of energy that meets the needs of "the present without compromising the ability of future generations to meet their own needs." [61] The solution lies in finding "sustainable energy sources and more efficient means of converting and utilizing energy."[62]

I believe that life is too short to spend our energy getting caught up in unimportant causes. Imagine devoting your time, talents and energy to a cause that you later learn is fruitless. It's like climbing a ladder only to discover that it was leaning

---

[61] Renewable Energy and Efficiency Partnership (British).
[62] *Sustainable Energy* by J. W. Tester, et al., from MIT Press.

against the wrong wall. Some things in life simply matter more than others.

Instead of trifling our time and energy on the mundane worries of the world, we must find a way to sustain our spiritual energy in the storms of derision and through the troubling times to come. As Christians we need to be able to tell the difference between what is crucial and what is merely convenient. We need to be able to discern between the fundamental and the fleeting. We need to sort through the sordid and secondary causes of our time and focus our efforts and energy on the greater good. Such a substantial effort will require a significant and sustainable source of power to support our undertaking. It will require that we become energetic and energized Christians.

Is our commitment to Christ fully charged with enough power and energy to withstand the adversity of our times? How do we gain sufficient energy to dedicate our lives to continuously following Christ and living consistently by our

Christian beliefs and values? From what source of power do we draw the energy to resist Satan's temptations? Do we have the energy to walk as Jesus walked when the road becomes too tough to travel? We can find and sustain all the renewable energy we need through the power of the Son!

Energized Christians put Christ first in their lives. Our egos tend to want to place us at the center of the universe where we expect everyone else to conform to our wants and desires. Our spiritual nature does not concur with such a mistaken notion. The central station of our lives belongs to God. Instead of expecting him to conform to our wishes, we should be bringing our lives into harmony with his will.

Energized Christians are those who make a consorted effort toward a total commitment to the cause of Christianity. We don't simply climb onto the strait and narrow path and stand there chit-chatting with each other about how fortunate we are. We perform the acts of Christianity that the gospel of Christ requires of us.

Energized Christians move forward with a clarity of faith, a love of God and a resoluteness in Christ. Having the energy to walk as Jesus walked means that we obey the two great commandments to love God and to love our neighbors. The first great commandment is: "Love the Lord your God with all your heart, with all your soul, and with all your mind." [63] To properly love God, we need to be willing to do the things he asks of us. Our actions, more than our words, will always reflect who we are and what we believe.

Energized Christians focus their attention on their distinct and certain purpose and never look back on their past problems or transgressions. To us the past is nothing more than an indication of our growth and our value in God's eyes.

---

[63] Matthew 22:37 (NET).

When a certain man approached Jesus and said to him, "I will follow you, Lord, but first let me say goodbye to my family." Jesus said to him, "No one who puts his hand to the plow and looks back is fit for the kingdom of God." [64] Digging a straight furrow requires that the person plowing keep his eyes fixed on a distinct point in front of him. If he looks back to see where he has been, he loses his reference point and increases his chance of drifting and plowing a crooked and uneven furrow. A more modern metaphor might be trying to drive a car while looking behind you to see what the kids in the backseat are doing. It would be an extremely dangerous and perhaps even deadly practice.

Energized Christians listen to the Holy Spirit. We persistently pursue its power and guidance. We pray for the energy and strength to conquer challenges and trials. Our hearts are set upon the things of heaven and that is where our treasure will be also.

---

[64] Luke 9:61, 62 (NET).

Energized Christians strengthen other believers and non-believers. We are eager to share the source of our spiritual energy and the purveyor of our happiness and hope. At the end of his life Patrick Henry remarked, "I have now disposed of all my property to my family.... There is one thing more I wish I could give them, and that is the Christian religion.... If they had that, and I had not given them one shilling, they would have been rich, and if they had not that, and I had given them all the world, they would be poor." [65]

Energized Christians put their beliefs into action. We anxiously perform good and noble deeds. We have ambition, we have desire, and we do all that we can possibly do to advance the work of God on Earth.

Energized Christians love one another, caring for refugees, orphans and widows or anyone in need of assistance.

---

[65] *The New Dictionary of Thoughts* [Garden City, New York: Standard Book Co., 1961], 561.

Energized Christians believe in a living God. Before he crossed the Jordan River, Joshua called the children of Israel, saying, "Come here and listen to the words of the Lord your God.... This is how you will know the living God is among you." [66]

Challenged by the giant Goliath, the young shepherd David courageously said to those near him, "...Who is this uncircumcised Philistine, that he defies the armies of the living God?" [67] Jeremiah also referred to the Lord as "the living God and the everlasting King." [68]

Energized Christians have complete conviction in a living God. Our only question is: Am I dedicated and committed to being an energetic, energized and "living" Christian?

An Energized Heart

The story of Esther from the Old Testament is a story of tension and suspense. Will Esther be

---

[66] Joshua 3:9, 10 (NET).
[67] 1 Samuel 17:26 (NET).
[68] Jeremiah 10:10 (KJV).

selected to become queen? Will Haman's anger and hatred for Esther's uncle cause him to annihilate all of Mordecai's people? The only possible way of stopping him is to engage the young, inexperienced Esther against the cunning Haman in a contest of intellect to influence the king.

Esther conveys to her uncle that she could be completely unsuccessful in her attempt. After all, the king hadn't sent for her for thirty days, and she would be risking her life by coming uninvited into the king's presence unless he extends his golden scepter to her. Mordecai answered her, not with soothing half-truths or comforting lies, but with the cold, hard truth: "Don't imagine that because you are part of the king's household you will be the one Jew who will escape. If you keep quiet at this time, liberation and protection for the Jews will appear from another source, while you and your father's household perish. It may very well be that you have achieved royal status for such a time as this." [69]

---

[69] Esther 4:14 (NET).

As the story goes, the king held out his scepter to Esther and she petitioned him on behalf of her people. Haman was hanged on the very gallows that he built for Mordecai, and the Jews received royal permission to stand against their enemies.

Mordecai's phrase, "for such a time as this" is very intriguing. What kind of time is our time? It is definitely a time of challenges. Christians are being murdered and beheaded in places around the entire world. In our homes, we are fighting the influences of drugs and disease, gangs and greed, tempests, violence, pollution, and a myriad of other trials and adversity. We certainly live in fearful times.

Esther may have felt secure in the king's household, but Mordecai pointed out that the edict of annihilation would not stop at the palace gates. Perhaps she could have denied her beliefs in an attempt to escape but escape and denial are the response of fear, not of faith.

Esther chose instead to respond with faith. She fasted three days to prepare herself spiritually to break the law of the kingdom and confront the king. She was well aware of the consequences because, as she stated, "If I perish, I perish." [70] She was willing to risk her life for her cause. Her real choice was not to live or to die; her choice was the kind of life she would live before she died.

We all have the same choice. What cause will we commit our energy to? Will we choose to live with faith, even in formidable times?

The choice is eloquently expressed by Maxwell Anderson in his play, *Joan of Lorraine*. As Joan of Arc awaits execution, she addresses her accusers with unassuming simplicity: "Every man gives his life for what he believes. Every woman gives her life for what she believes. Sometimes people believe in little or nothing, nevertheless they give up their lives to that little or nothing. One life is all we have, and we live it as we believe in living it, and then it's gone. But to surrender what you are, and live

---

[70] Esther 4:16 (NET).

without belief—that is more terrible than dying—more terrible than dying young." [71]

We also live in troubling times. Our strength, our shield, and our defense must be in our individual witness of Christ. We must develop an energized heart to sustain the internal strength to face the challenges of our day with faith and courage, instead of with fear and faltering. We need to give our hearts over to Jesus so that he becomes the light of our lives and the touchstone by which we measure every action, every word, and every thought. Only Jesus Christ is uniquely qualified to provide the hope, confidence, and strength we need to overcome the world and rise above our human failings.

Many of us perhaps do not even think about our witness and testimony of Jesus. We may just have faith in what our parents taught us. Or perhaps we rely on the strength and conviction of a spouse. Some of us might only have faith in the teachings of

---

[71] Anderson, Maxwell, *Joan of Lorraine: A Play in Two Acts* (Washington, D.C.: Anderson House, 1947), 127.

a local pastor or in the church we belong to but have neglected to build our own faith in Christ. Under normal circumstances these are all good, loving and worthy voices to rely on. Unfortunately, not all fathers are faithful, not all spouses are supportive and not all churches nurture our individual, spiritual needs.

If, ultimately, we place our faith in fleeting figures and impermanent places we risk losing the sustainable spirituality that will provide strength and energy to our souls. We need to stay connected to the power of the Son. We need to hearken to his voice—to seek it, to listen carefully so that we can distinguish it from all other voices, and to pay close attention to its message.

If we explore the Word of God, if we converse intimately with our God through personal prayer, constantly asking, "What would Jesus say or do in my situation," then, when a faith-based decision needs to be made, we will know the proper principle to follow and we will not be swayed by the loud, competing worldly voices of the faithless fanatics that surround us.

Mother Teresa is a great example of a woman with an energized heart. In Bangalore she was once criticized for "spoiling" the poor because she so generously dispensed food and goods to them. Mother Teresa persuasively responded by saying, "If I spoil the poor, you and the other sisters spoil the rich in your select schools. And Almighty God is the first to spoil us. Does he not give freely to all of us? Then why should I not imitate my God and give freely to the poor what I have received freely?" [72]

Mother Teresa's clever comeback powerfully and proficiently presented her accusers with a principle of Christianity they both believed in. Mother Teresa's words persuasively reminded them to listen to their own Christian hearts and ask themselves, "What would Jesus have done?"

---

[72] Jose Luis Gonzalez-Galado and Janet N. Playfoot, *My Life for the Poor: Mother Teresa of Calcutta* (San Francisco: Harper & Row, Publishers, 1985), 31.

We live in fearsome times. We need to confront the challenges of our days with the sustained strength of an energized heart. We need to cultivate such a close relationship with Christ and recognize his voice from among all the other voices that clamor around us. Then we can act with the integrity of an energized Christian.

During the Revolutionary War, on May 19, 1780 darkness fell at noon. When the sun was at its peak, an atmospheric marvel brought the day to an early and unexpected close. People panicked suspecting that the end of the world had come. [73]

---

[73] New England's "Dark Day" occurred on May 19, 1780, when an unusual darkening of the sky was seen during the daytime in New England and parts of Canada. The primary cause of the event is believed to have been a combination of smoke from forest fires, a thick fog, and heavy cloud cover. The day became so dark that candles were necessary to be able to see at noon. This dark cover did not disperse until the following night. For several days before the dark day, the sun appeared red and the sky appeared yellow. Soot collected in rivers and water, suggesting the presence of smoke. Also, when the night actually did come, the moon also appeared red. A New England rain that same morning indicated that cloud cover was present. The most likely cause of the darkness was smoke from a massive forest fire. Researchers examining tree scar damage in

At Hartford, Connecticut, the State Legislature was in session. The meeting of the Lower House came to a halt in astonishment and wonder. A motion of adjournment was made in the State Senate as legislators prepared to meet the Day of Judgment. But the motion was opposed by Abraham Davenport, a friend and advisor to George Washington.

He stood and addressed his legislative associates with courageous logic: "I am against this adjournment. The Day of Judgment is either approaching or it is not. If it is not, there is no cause for adjournment. If it is, I choose to be found doing my duty. I wish, therefore, that candles may be brought." [74]

We each face this same choice every day of our existence. We can be found in panic and dismay or we can be found doing our Christian duty, even in

---

what is now Algonquin Provincial Park in Ontario, Canada attribute the dark day to a large fire in that area.

[74] Thomas, Lowell, *The Day the Sun Went Out,* in A New Treasury of Words to Live by, edited by William Nichols (New York: Simon and Schuster, 1957), 59-60.

the darkest times, with the light of Christ shining as our candle while we work.

An Energized Religion

The word "religion" has recently taken on a somewhat negative connotation. We hear people proclaim that they see themselves as spiritual but not religious. Perhaps they see religion as being part of a human organization or corporation while they see spirituality more as an innate connection with God.

The Bible is the greatest religious text of all time and yet, the word "religion" appears a scant three times in this entire voluminous manuscript. The word is first used by Paul in his defense before King Agrippa: "According to the strictest party of our religion, I lived as a Pharisee." [75] Of the three sects of the Jews, Pharisees, Sadducees, and Essenes, Paul was a Pharisee, the strictest of the three in ritualistic religious performances.

---

[75] Acts 26:5 (NET).

The word religion appears a second time in Paul's letter to the Galatians. Paul wrote, "You have heard of my way of living in time past in the Jews' religion, how that beyond measure I persecuted the assembly of God, and ravaged it." [76] Most of us are familiar with Paul's persecutions of those who professed to be Christians. Paul explains that he had practiced the religion of his fathers—a Hebrew heritage of resolute rules, staunch laws, and tenacious traditions. These pitiless practices caused him to harshly harass the followers of Christ. In both cases, Paul uses the word religion to refer to the rules of practice rather than to the doctrines or beliefs.

The final use of the word religion is by James writing to the twelve tribes. In his letter James writes, "If someone thinks he is religious yet does not bridle his tongue, and so deceives his heart, his religion is futile." [77] James uses the term religion in the same way as Paul, as something ceremonial or

---

[76] Galatians 1:13 (WEB).
[77] James 1:26 (NET).

ritualistic. If we are ritualistic in our behavior, he suggests, but don't watch what we say, then our rituals are meaningless. Rituals by themselves are powerless. It is our devotion to God that energizes our religious practices.

James emphatically explains what he considers "pure and undefiled religion," as opposed to the ritualistic worship and powerless practices portrayed by Paul. "Pure and undefiled religion before God the Father is this: to care for orphans and widows in their misfortune and to keep oneself unstained by the world." [78] His words are simple and unpretentious, yet their meaning is profound.

To "care for orphans and widows" reminds us to be compassionate to our fellowmen. Just as Jesus frequently taught that we should love our neighbor as ourselves, [79] James uses the fatherless and widows as examples for expressing compassionate service to others and a true and energetic devotion to God.

---

[78] James 1:27 (NET).
[79] Matthew 22:39 (NET).

The second half of James' definition of pure religion is to keep ourselves "unstained by the world." Being unstained by the world means being free from the pollution of sin. Paul's writing to the Romans emphasizes the same practice: "Do not be conformed to this present world, but be transformed by the renewing of your mind, so that you may test and approve what is the will of God – what is good and well-pleasing and perfect."

The pure religion that James portrays is a powerful devotion to God, energized by love and compassion for others and strengthened by freedom from sin. In other words, energized religion requires we refrain from doing wrong while purposefully and persistently performing acts of kindness and assistance to others. Matthew said it like this, "Just as you did it for one of the least of these brothers or sisters of mine, you did it for me." [80] Our energized religion should portray the same attributes of service to God and to humanity.

---

[80] Matthew 25:40 (NET).

We must not believe that we are not innately religious. Spiritual sustainability will require that we practice an energetic and pure religion in both appearance and in actuality. Our love of purity, decency, honesty, compassion and kindness is the undeniable confirmation of our innate spirituality. We can encourage its growth and development through devotion to God, demonstrated by love and compassion for others, coupled with unworldliness. Performing kindnesses for others and avoiding unrighteous influences will do more to sustain our spirituality than any ritualistic performance which is devoid of true devotion.

CHAPTER SEVEN

THREE PILLARS OF SPIRITUAL SUSTAINABILITY

The term "sustainability" originates from the Latin word *sustinere*, which means to hold up. Sustain can mean maintain, support, or endure. Since around the early 1980s, the expression "sustainability" has conveyed a sense of human sustainability on planet Earth. The result has been a widely quoted definition of sustainability as "sustainable development that meets the needs of the present without compromising the ability of future generations to meet their own needs." [81]

In 2005, the World Summit on Social Development identified three sustainable development objectives. These objectives, known as the three pillars of sustainability, include economic development, social development and environmental protection. They serve as a common ground for numerous sustainability standards and are mutually reinforcing.

The terminology may be simple and vague, but sustainability is seen as something that improves the quality of human life while supporting future eco-systems. But sustainability is also a specific call to action, a task in progress or a "journey," and therefore, a process.

Sustainability implies responsible and proactive decision-making coupled with innovation that minimizes negative impact while maintaining a

---

[81] The Brundtland Commission of the United Nations on March 20, 1987.

balance between ecological resilience, economic prosperity, political justice and cultural vibrancy to ensure a desirable planet for all species now and in the future.

The development of sustainable spirituality also requires responsible and proactive progress toward specific objectives. The three sustainable spirituality objectives include prayer, study and service. They are the common ground for developing spiritual strength and are also mutually reinforcing.

Developing sustainable spirituality is accomplished only through deliberate effort and a specific call to action. Developing sustainable spirituality and attuning ourselves to the highest influences of heaven is unquestionably not an easy process. It takes time and often involves an exerted effort. It does not happen by chance, but is accomplished through deliberate determination.

Paul exhausted his life in teaching and encouraging spiritual growth throughout the distant missions of the Roman Empire and beyond. He often used examples and expressions from athletic contests to convey his argument. He proposed that a Christian successfully obeying God's commandments is comparable to an athlete winning a contest. Similarities in training, exertion, obeying rules, personal discipline, and the desire to win exist between the two.

In writing to the Corinthians, Paul says in effect, "Don't you know that those who run in a race all run, but one receives the prize? Run like that, that you may win. Every man who strives in the games exercises self-control in all things. Now they do it to receive a corruptible crown, but we an incorruptible. I therefore run like that, as not uncertainly." [82]

He comparably wrote to his friend, Timothy, "I have competed well; I have finished the race; I have kept the faith! Finally the crown of righteousness is reserved for me. The Lord, the righteous Judge, will award it to me in that day – and

---

[82] 1 Corinthians 9:24-26 (WEB).

not to me only, but also to all who have set their affection on his appearing." [83]

In Paul's day, an athletic contest was at times a hand-to-hand confrontation to the death. Considering this extreme nature of the competition, Paul wrote,

"Clothe yourself with the full armor of God so that you may be able to stand against the schemes of the devil. For our struggle is not against flesh and blood but against the rulers, against the powers, against the world rulers of this darkness, against the spiritual forces of evil in high places.

"For this reason take up the full armor of God so that you may be able to stand your ground on the evil day, and having done everything, to stand.

"Stand firm therefore, by fastening the belt of truth around your waist, by putting on the breastplate of righteousness,

---

[83] 2 Timothy 4:7, 8 (NET).

"By fitting your feet with the preparation that comes from the good news of peace,

"And in all of this, by taking up the shield of faith with which you can extinguish all the flaming arrows of the evil one.

"And take the helmet of salvation and the sword of the Spirit, which is the word of God.

"With every prayer and petition, pray at all times in the Spirit, and to this end be alert, with all perseverance and requests for all the saints." [84]

God created us with magnificent minds capable of learning and spiritual strength which may be amplified in proportion to our obedience to God. The closer we are to God; the closer God is to us. Our convictions can be clearer, life's pleasures can be greater, and we can lose all desire to sin.

Part of the struggle as we strive to acquire sustainable spirituality is the feeling that it is too far

---

[84] Ephesians 6:11-18 (NET).

out of reach. We may feel that we fall too short of the prize, but we can capitalize on our strengths. Starting right where we are today, we can seek the happiness that is found in pursuing the spiritual things of God.

The place to begin is here. The time to start is now. The effort can be simply one step at a time. A simple prayer silently spoken from the heart, a page of scripture studied and applied to our personal circumstances, a small act of kindness performed for someone in need will move us in the direction of our spiritual objective. God will lead us along and we will, by our persistent progress, approach the glorious prize.

Every person on earth can make spiritual progress. The gospel of Jesus Christ is more than a powerful code of ethics, more than an ideal social order, more than a program of positive thinking or self-improvement. It is a divine plan for spiritual growth and sustainability. It is the saving power of the Lord Jesus Christ. With faith in Christ we can move a step at a time, improving as we go, asking for strength, refining our attitudes and our ambitions, until we find ourselves securely in the fold of the Good Shepherd.

There is no doubt that it will require discipline and training, exertion and strength. But as the Apostle Paul said, "I can do all things through Christ who strengthens me." [85]

At a decisive moment in the battle of Waterloo, a concerned courier rode up to the Duke of Wellington to inform him that, unless they retreated immediately, they would fall before the impending assault of the French army. The Duke replied, "Stand firm!"

"But we shall perish," argued the officer.

"Stand firm!" the Duke again responded.

"You'll find us there!" replied the courier and he galloped away.

---

[85] Philippians 4:13 (WEB).

The British were victorious that day as a result of the Duke's determination and the loyalty of his soldiers. [86] Another battle with even bleaker consequences is being fought today. It is the battle for the souls of humanity. The outcome similarly hinges on the steadiness of the soldiers. The call of the Commander is still, "Stand firm!"

We must stand firm and remain true to the kingdom of God as we live our Christian beliefs in the quiet commonplace of our daily lives. We can do so as we learn to rely on the three pillars of sustainable spirituality.

---

[86] Baxendale, Walter, ed., *Dictionary of Anecdote, Incident, Illustrative Fact* [New York, 1889], 225.

CHAPTER EIGHT

THE PILLAR OF PERSONAL PRAYER

The moral pollution index in our society is rising. The devil is on the loose. Without the sustaining infusion of spiritual power that comes through communion with God, Christians are no stronger than anyone else. We cannot resist the incessant pull of immorality. We cannot elude the desensitization from the daily doses of violence and cruelty on our own. We are all vulnerable to satanic influences and too susceptible to confront the enemy alone.

But we can refine and purify our lives through the regular practice of prayer. We can call on God when we are overjoyed or when we are overwhelmed. We can voice our souls' deepest desires when we have been blessed or when we have been humbled to the dust. We can stand with confidence in his mighty cause, knowing that, no matter the enormity of the ranks of the enemy, God is with us.

As Christians, our prayer life—how often we pray, how earnestly we pray, and how trustingly we pray—is an unerring measure of our sustainable spirituality. Prayer keeps us from sinning; sinning keeps us from prayer. We cannot climb the mountain of spirituality without raising our hearts and voices in fervent prayer to God.

As we become more prayerful, we develop a greater sustainable faith in God, trusting and relying on spiritual powers that are much greater than our own mortal power. By providing us access to an all-powerful God, prayer builds and sustains spiritual strength far beyond our limited abilities. We can do plenty on our own but there are some things that can only be accomplished with divine assistance.

The powerful gift of prayer permits us to cultivate a close relationship with God and Christ. Through prayer we convey our deepest needs, our personal earnest feelings, our heart-felt desires to God and then ask sincerely for his help.

To a large extent, our lives are the product of the friendships we foster. The more we develop a close association with God, the greater our characteristics will become. We will develop the capacity to rise above the petty and insignificant trivialities of our mortal sins and fears. Just as a continual association with degrading influences will adversely affect us, a persistent connection with God will elevate and improve us.

By engaging our hearts and minds in sincere prayer, God, through his Holy Spirit, will infuse our souls with purpose and a greater personal power and influence. As we gain greater strength from an omnipotent Being, our spirits will become instilled with a sustainable spiritual energy.

Some prayers are simple, joyful expressions of gratitude. Some are deep pleadings for our heavy sorrows to be lifted. And some prayers are impassioned struggles for a greater spiritual connection with God. Some prayers pour freely from our hearts while others require strenuous and disciplined effort. Jacob wrestled with an angel throughout the entire night until he obtained his desired blessing from God. [87]

Jesus understood this powerful principle of prayer as he poured his heart out to his Father on the Mount of Olives. "And in his anguish," Luke tells us, "he prayed more earnestly." [88] What a marvelous and noteworthy statement! The Son of God "prayed more earnestly."

Jesus did all things correctly. His every word was true and his every deed was proper. He was the only perfect being to walk the dusty paths of planet Earth. And yet, Jesus Christ, the Son of God "prayed

---

[87] See Genesis 32:24-32.
[88] Luke 22:44 (NET).

more earnestly." His example shows us that not all prayers are alike. Greater need requires more serious and faith-filled persuading before the throne of God.

Of course, not all prayers will require such a consorted effort on our part, but some "thorns in the flesh" [89] will demand prayers of significant strength and intensity. Just as Jacob did not wrestle with God in every prayer every day, our prayers will not all involve the full, soul-wrenching effort required for specific troublesome times. But if we are willing to invest the time and expend the energy to pray more earnestly, then miracles will begin to take place in our lives.

Our prayers will then become edifying and instructive, and God can show us many important and pertinent things. Paul taught that "the Spirit helps us in our weakness, for we do not know how we should pray, but the Spirit himself intercedes for us with inexpressible groanings." [90]

---

[89] See 2 Corinthians 12:7-10.
[90] Romans 8:26 (NET).

In other words, when we are attentive, the Spirit of the Lord can help us pray for things we might not have thought of on our own, deeply spiritual things beyond our physical human desires. We could find our words surpassing our thoughts as the Spirit assists us to pray for people, possibilities and prospects in ways that may astound us.

We could encounter obstacles in developing such a spiritually sustaining communion with God that will inhibit us from enjoying the relationship that we would like to have. When we pray to God we have no one to impress and no judgment to fear. He knows all things, including the desires of our hearts. Therefore, we should only speak the words that we truly feel.

Our prayers should be plain and simple. We should just ask for what we want the same as we would ask an Earthly parent, "Hey Dad, can I borrow the car tonight?"

In Shakespeare's play, *Hamlet*, Claudius ceased praying because his heart was simply not in his prayers. He said,

"My words fly up, my thoughts remain below;
Words without thoughts never to heaven go." [91]

Physical distractions and concerns can be a hindrance to effective prayer. It can be helpful if we slow down, stop what we're doing, and sit quietly before we approach God. Listening to inspiring music or reading a few verses of the Bible can help us contemplate and reflect before prayer.

Duplicity is another roadblock to an effective prayer. If we are sinful throughout the day we can't expect to pray effectively at night. Henry Ward Beecher said, "It is not well for a man to pray cream and live skim milk." Today we see a greater tendency for people to pray skim milk and not even live that. The more faithful we are in keeping God's

---

[91] Shakespeare, William, *Hamlet*, Act 3, Scene 3.

commandments and putting him first, the wider he opens the doors of communication with us.

Another deficiency is praying without much thought, reflection, or devotion. When our prayers are only a spasmodic cry for help at the time of crisis, then our petitions become entirely selfish. God is not a repairman we call on only in emergencies. We should remember to pray in the good times as well as the bad, and not only when all other support has failed and we feel desperate. Remember, if you only pray when you're in trouble, you're in trouble!

Answers to Prayers

Understand that God answers prayers. We haven't really developed a sustainable level of faith and spirituality until we understand that we can pray, we can listen and we can know when our prayers are answered. We can get close to God. He isn't an absentee parent. He will be as close to us as we allow him to be.

The time will come in the life of each of us when we pray but seem not to receive the answer we seek. God is willing to give, and will give, all that he sees is good for us, even when he doesn't give us all we ask for. We should recognize and follow the example Jesus set when we petition God and say, "not my will but yours be done." [92] And then remember, sometimes the answer is no.

Receiving answers to our prayer requires we make a sincere effort. Our intention should be real, the desire of our hearts should be sincere and we should have the faith in Christ to request and receive what we seek.

Receiving answers is facilitated when we have a deep feeling of spiritual need. It is more than just saying words and receiving answers. It is through a sense of humility and dependence on God that we can have answers to our prayers.

---

[92] Luke 22:42 (NET).

Answers will come to the extent that we are diligent in following God's law. In humility we should ask, as Paul did, "Lord, what wilt thou have me to do?" [93] With undaunted courage we should say, as Samuel did, "Speak, Lord, for your servant is listening." [94] Then, when God does tell you what to do, you had better have the faith to do it or you had better not ask again.

Sustainable spirituality comes from prayer. Prayer is our passport to spiritual power. Prayer doesn't ever promise us freedom from adversity and affliction. It does, instead, offer us a channel of communication to seek divine help and spiritual guidance.

---

[93] Acts 9:6 (KJV).
[94] 1 Samuel 3:9 (NET).

CHAPTER NINE

THE PILLAR OF PERSONAL STUDY

The word of God is often an instrument of re-birth and the means by which we become new creatures in Christ. Saul of Tarsus was undoubtedly touched by Stephen's testimony as he reflected on those words while traveling to Damascus. [95]

Paul later wrote about the importance of personal human testimony:

"For everyone who calls on the name of the Lord shall be saved.

---

[95] See Acts 7; 9.

"How are they to call on one they have not believed in? And how are they to believe in one they have not heard of? And how are they to hear without someone preaching to them.

"And how are they to preach unless they are sent? As it is written, 'How timely is the arrival of those who proclaim the good news'

"...Consequently faith comes from what is heard, and what is heard comes through the preached word of Christ." [96]

The Bible is a powerful witness for Jesus Christ and his gospel. In addition, it is of significant importance considering what we can learn from the experiences of the other people in it as well. A review of the historical events in the Bible allows us to see a reflection of our own lives. We can compare circumstances and conditions in our time with those in relevant segments of Biblical history and predict with a sense of accuracy the consequences of our

---

[96] Romans 10:13-15, 17 (NET).

own human behavior. We can gain insight into how to warrant God's blessings as well as how to avoid the catastrophes that frequently followed the people in Biblical times.

Human writing may be witty and sometimes even wise; but the word of God touches the core of what matters most and goes straight to the heart of life's most important issues. There is great virtue and great power in the word of God. People have completely turned their lives around and become converted simply by reading the pure witness of the word.

The power of the Bible is not in its sophistication nor in its appeal to the wise. Its sustaining power emanates from God to its readers. "Our gospel did not come to you merely in words, but in power and in the Holy Spirit and with deep conviction." [97] It transcends the interests of style and delivers substance instead.

---

[97] 1 Thessalonians 1:5 (NET).

Paul told the Corinthians, "I did not come with superior eloquence or wisdom as I proclaimed the testimony of God. For I decided to be concerned about nothing among you except Jesus Christ, and him crucified. And I was with you in weakness and in fear and in much trembling. My conversation and my preaching were not with persuasive words of wisdom, but with a demonstration of the Spirit and with power, so that your faith would not be based on human wisdom but on the power of God." [98]

The word of God by itself is so powerful that gospel teachers do not need to shoulder the burden of converting their listeners. With all of the reading, studying, preparing, praying, organizing, and presenting a minister or a teacher may do, the spiritual lesson is presented by the Spirit. He is the true teacher and the sole converter, conveying the word of truth into our hearts and minds. This is how the Spirit sustains our faith and strengthens our

---

[98] 1 Corinthians 2:1-5 (NET).

testimony—through the power and conviction of the word of God.

We all respond differently to the word of truth, and sometimes we are unaware of the effect of our reading or the good that it does. Stephen [99] succumbed to a cruel death at the hands of wicked men. (I don't imagine that it is an easy thing to die for our convictions, but death must be much sweeter for those who die bearing fervent witness of Christ.) And so Stephen was put to death. But the testament lived on. Faith came to Paul who heard the word of God preached by a faithful testator for Christ.

When we immerse ourselves in the Bible regularly and consistently, our level of sustainable spirituality increases significantly. Our testimony of the truth will grow. Our commitment to the cause of Christ will be strengthened.

Increased integrity, the power to resist temptation, daily guidance and direction, are a few

---

[99] See Acts 7.

of the promises God offers us when we feast on his word. If God tells us that these things will come through his word, then those blessings will be ours. Blessings are found in the Holy Scriptures. By accepting the word of God we can navigate through the mists of darkness and come to Christ.

Profiting from Bible Study

The Bible offers us fascinating vicarious experiences. Of the billions who live on earth no one can walk with God like Adam did. We don't have the privilege and opportunity to speak with God like Moses did. But the Bible is available to nearly every soul, and, through it, we can become personally acquainted with God and his Son Jesus Christ.

All through the Bible every weakness and every strength of humanity is vividly portrayed. So are the subsequent rewards and punishments. The Bible clarifies the good. It also illuminates evil. We can learn the lessons of life easily when we see the good and poor choices of others in the past. The faithfulness of the followers of God under stress, temptation and persecution can serve to strengthen and sustain our own personal resolve.

Studying Job, we learn to keep faith through the greatest of adversities. Reading how Joseph, engulfed in the luxuries of Egypt and tempted by Potiphar's wife, resisted all the powers of darkness should certainly sustain us against similar sin.

Examining Peter's growth as the catalyst of the Good News advances him from an uncultured and unlearned fisherman into a great organizer, theologian and teacher will sustain our courage and conviction that nothing but ourselves can stop our spiritual progress.

Witnessing the forbearance and fortitude of Paul in giving his life to Christ gives us added courage when we feel injured and tried. Paul was beaten and imprisoned, stoned and robbed, shipwrecked and nearly drowned. He was the victim of false friends and underhanded associates. At times starving, choking, freezing, poorly clothed,

Paul remained consistent in his service. He never faltered after his witness came to him.

Watching Saul progress from a donkey tender to the king of Israel and then seeing his arrogance and pride drive him down from his throne to the tent of Endor's witch like a man gone mad; to see him defeated in battle, his decapitated head displayed for his enemies to spit at, will certainly teach us a valuable lesson on pride and arrogance.

The Bible is very direct in its approach. It is tough on the rebellious and wicked but soothing and healing to the repentant sinner.

Jesus advised us to "study the scriptures thoroughly because you think in them you possess eternal life." [100] In Jesus' life we discover the valuable qualities of goodness, strength, self-control and godliness. By studying this great Book, we can capture some of those qualities for ourselves. These vital scriptures are the essence of courage, faith, and

---

[100] John 5:39 (NET).

fortitude. They portray perseverance, great sacrifice, and super-human accomplishments. They contain stories of intrigue, vengeance, adversity, war and murder; of idolatry, miracles, revelations, and prophecy. The Bible is life at its best and at its worst. It carries us through colossal crisis and then engulfs us in God's great love.

We shouldn't overestimate our Biblical education. Many of us have a few favorite verses of scripture at our somewhat immediate mental disposal, drifting aimlessly somewhere in our minds. This creates the illusion that we know and understand much of the Bible. At some point in our lives, we really need to uncover more of these hidden truths for ourselves. If we want to become spiritually sustainable, we need to make the lessons of the Bible a regular and well-known part of our lives.

If we enthusiastically pursue a study of the Bible with a conscientious and resolute effort, we will find answers to our problems and peace in our hearts. We will feel the Holy Spirit expanding our awareness with new and greater insights. The doctrines of Christ will become more meaningful and certain and we will gain greater wisdom to direct and determine the course of our lives. We will also become a light and a strength to non-believers.

Access to the Bible requires responsibility for its teachings. God isn't kidding when he tells us that "to whoever much is given, of him will much be required." [101] We don't receive eternal life without becoming "doers of the word," [102] valiant in obeying God's law. We can't become "doers" without first being "hearers." God's word has always been given to those who have "eyes to see" and "ears to hear." As "hearers" we can't simply wait for random pieces of information to find their way into our minds, we need to seek and study.

God's voice is clear and unmistakable. If you haven't already done so, I ask you to begin now to study the scriptures in earnest. Neglecting Bible

---

[101] Luke 12:48 (NET).
[102] James 1:22 (NET).

study will certainly rob us of the strength we need to sustain our spirituality.

CHAPTER TEN

THE PILLAR OF SERVICE TO OTHERS

When the Apostle Paul declared that "love is patient and kind," [103] he wasn't just talking about being nice to one another and smiling at each other all day long. He was revealing to us the core and heart of Christian living. Kindness without love is not kindness at all. It's patronage, condescension and snobbery. Anyone who has been the recipient of this type of "kindness" knows they are better off without

---

[103] 1 Corinthians 13:4 (NET).

it. But when reinforced with love, kind deeds create refreshing connections and build friendly bonds.

Mother Teresa tells us that "it is not very often things [the poor] need. What they need much more is what we offer them. In these twenty years of work amongst the people, I have come more and more to realize that it is being unwanted that is the worst disease that any human being can ever experience. Nowadays we have found medicine for leprosy and lepers can be cured. There's medicine for TB and consumptives can be cured. For all kinds of diseases there are medicines and cures. But for being unwanted, except there are willing hands to serve and there's a loving heart to love, I don't think this terrible disease can ever be cured." [104]

---

[104] Quoted in Malcolm Muggeridge, *Something Beautiful for God: Mother Teresa of Calcutta* (New York: Walker and Company/Phoenix Press, 1971, large print edition 1984), 96.

Simple human kindness from the heart is the cure. Kindness is not complicated. It's little things, done consistently, with a cumulative impact.

Often we feel we don't have the time or the resources to make any real and significant difference in someone else's life. But, no matter how small or seemingly insignificant the effort, we can all do what we can. In a compilation of letters to God, a young girl wrote, "Dear God, I am sending you a penny to give to a kid poorer than me. Love, Donna." [105] Well, a penny certainly isn't very much. Most of us wouldn't even stoop to pick one up off the sidewalk. But this simple act of generosity reveals the kindness of this little girl's heart. There's nothing insignificant about that!

I once read a story about a man on a bus who was presented with the opportunity to perform a kind service to a woman in need. The woman slouched in her seat near the front of the bus. She

---

[105] Marshall, Eric and Hample, Stuart, comps. *Children's Letters to God,* enl. ed. (New York: Pocket Books, 1975).

was visibly weary and overwhelmed. Her unkempt hair lay matted against her dirty face. It was the middle of winter but this poor woman was wearing nothing more than a flimsy cotton dress and a blanket with torn-out arm holes. It was obvious that she was in desperate hardship.

The man on the bus wanted to help her and pondered over what he could do. Maybe he could direct her to a shelter and they could help her. Her plight and problems appeared too overwhelmingly complex for this one man to handle. As he thought of, and subsequently dismissed, possible solutions to the poor woman's predicament, the bus came to a stop.

Another young man, in neat but inexpensive attire, stood up to exit the bus. It wasn't until the bus had started on its way again that the first man noticed what this young man had done. He had slipped off his black knit gloves and laid them on poor woman's lap. [106]

That young man couldn't solve all the poor woman's worries and troubles nor did he try, but he saw her cold, red hands and knew he could do something about them. And he did it.

Kindness is no more complicated than that and we are all in a position to do similar kind deeds for one another every day. Small acts of kindness ripple like water in a pond except, in the case of kindness, the ripples grow stronger as they go.

Kindness is self-sustaining and a Christian heart is impulsively kind. Kindness creates a confident and caring association with another human being, even with a stranger whom we may never see again. It is amazing to see how quickly Christ's love can fill our hearts from even a tiny act

---

[106] Sisley, Jr., John H., untitled anecdote *in The Prince of Peace Is Born* (pamphlet) (Carmel, NY: Guideposts Associates, 1991).

of kindness. It is deeply empowering! Kindness really is its own reward.

When the Dalai Lama was asked to describe the Tibetan religion, he said, "My religion is very simple. My religion is kindness." [107] But kindness is also the heart of the Christian religion.

Christian kindness comes from the heart. It is kindness for kindness' sake alone, not because we're expecting some great payoff or because we want others to notice how righteous and good we are. Christians should never expect any external reward.

Wilma Hepker studied burnout in community volunteers and made this powerful observation: "If we're willing to help only perfect people, we might as well shut down everything right now because there aren't any perfect people out there to help.

"No, if you're going to survive volunteering, you can't do so because you think the people you're

---

[107] Dalai Lama, as quoted in Editors of Canari Press, *Random Acts of Kindness* (Berkeley, CA: Conari Press, 1993), 20.

helping deserve it. You can't help people because they'll thank you. You have to help them because Christ loves them and He's loving them through you. You volunteer because in doing so, you represent Christ to them in the here and now—even if they don't see Him in you." [108]

We've all experienced kindness and unkindness and consequently, we can easily recognize how it feels when someone is being kind to us. Hopefully, we also recognize the subtle feeling in our own hearts that occurs when we have been kind to someone else. It's a feeling that is hard to describe but easy to identify. Very little in this life is as comforting during times of heartache as receiving the kindness of others—unless, of course, it's being able to perform some random kindness ourselves. We've all heard that, "If you want to feel better yourself, do something for someone else." This is literally true.

---

[108] Hepker, Wilma, *"Survival Tactics for Volunteers"* Signs of the Times, October 1993, 13.

We should always offer kindness wherever we can, even when fairness does not require it. We should live our lives with greater attention to the love and hope and compassion Jesus Christ displayed toward others. We can always treat each other with a little more kindness, a little more courtesy, and with greater humility, patience and forgiveness.

Paul told the Corinthians how they could recognize a true representative of Christ: "By purity, by knowledge, by patience, by benevolence (kindness), by the Holy Spirit, by genuine love." [109] The world today needs more Christ-like love and kindness. It is an invitation that we can all accept. We should never allow any occasion to be kind to simply pass us by. Kindness has an infinite ability to fill our lives with profound meaning and deep significance.

---

[109] 2 Corinthians 6:6 (NET).

CHAPTER ELEVEN

A FOUNDATION OF CHARITY

Jesus gave us "a new commandment" which identifies us as his disciples. He directed us "to love one another.... Everyone will know by this that you are my disciples." [110] The love that we carry for the human family is the same love Jesus extends to everyone. It is the loftiest height the human soul can reach and the deepest utterance of the human heart.

It is difficult to assign a specific definition to the English word *love*. The expression, "I love pizza"

---

[110] John 13:34, 35 (NET).

is very different from the expression, "I love my wife" (or at least it should be!) and yet, we use the same word in expressing both emotions. The ancient Greek used four distinct words to define the concept of love; *Agape, Phileo, Storge,* and *Eros.* Ancient Greek is the language of the New Testament.

Agape is the highest form of love. It is the kind of love that comes from God. It is a divine love, a perfect, pure, and self-sacrificing love. The scripture, "God is love" [111] refers to agape. The King James Version of the Bible translates the word *agape* as *charity.* [112] Agape, or charity, goes beyond simple feelings and emotions.

To remain spiritually sustainable, our sullen and sad world needs this pure love of Christ. The standard of charity is the only way this world will ever experience peace. If our hearts are filled with charity, we will be kinder to each other, gentler and more forgiving. We will be slower to anger and more

---

[111] 1 John 4:8 (NET).
[112] See 1 Corinthians 13 (KJV).

willing to help. We will extend the hand of friendship and withhold the hand of retribution. We will love one another with genuine compassion the same way that God loves us. We will walk more resolutely the path that Jesus walked.

All of us want a more peaceful world, with peaceful communities, neighborhoods and families. Securing and sustaining such a peaceful setting involves learning to love each other, our friends and our enemies alike. A peaceful world requires the pure love of Christ. It entails loving each other with the same self-sacrificing love Paul refers to as agape or charity.

A sure indication of our spiritual sustainability is our increased capability to love. Pure love is centered in God. John wrote that "God is love, and the one who resides in love resides in God, and God resides in him." [113] Pure love can only come from a pure source and that source is God. God loves purely, absolutely, and perfectly. John

---

[113] 1 John 4:16 (NET).

understood that the reason we love God is because he first loved us. [114]

The greatest indication of God's love is the gift of his Beloved Son. God "so loved the world, that he gave his one and only Son, that whoever believes in him should not perish, but have eternal life." [115] Anyone who has had the burden of sin removed, the heaviness of guilt lifted, and the suffering of resentment, anger, or agony relieved by the healing hand of Christ knows the purifying, cleansing feeling of the pure love of Christ.

Our love for God will grow as we acknowledge his goodness, as we gain greater awareness of his involvement in our lives, as we recognize his influence in everything honorable, good and worthy in our individual circumstances and situations. All our personal desires, whether physical or spiritual, should be set in the love of God.

---

[114] 1 John 4:10, 19 (NET).
[115] John 3:16 (WEB).

Jesus acknowledged the destitute and the deprived; infants and widows; farmers and fishermen; shepherds and goat herders. He recognized strangers and foreigners; the prominent wealthy and the powerful politicians; even the unfavorable Pharisees and scribes.

He cared for the poor, the hungry and the sick. He blessed the crippled, the blind and the deaf. He forgave people burdened with sin. He taught love which was demonstrated by an unselfish service to others. No one was ever denied Christ's love.

Sustainable spiritualty requires us to purify our inner feelings, to change our hearts, to make our outward actions and appearance conform to what we say we believe and feel inside. It requires we become true disciples of Christ.

In the scope of our Christian lives and in a world filled with so much need and sorrow, we all have ample opportunity to someday hear Christ say to us, "For I was hungry and you gave me food, I was thirsty and you gave me something to drink, I was a stranger, and you invited me in, I was naked and you gave me clothing, I was sick and you took care of me, I was in prison and you visited me."

At that moment perhaps we will wonder when did we do these kindnesses for our Lord. We may turn to him confused and ask, "Lord, when did we see you hungry and feed you, or thirsty and give you something to drink, when did we see you a stranger and invite you in, or naked and clothe you? When did we see you in prison and visit you?"

Then Jesus will answer us, "Just as you did it for one of the least of these brothers or sisters of mine, you did it for me." [116]

Random acts of kindness, good deeds, and works of faith are much more meaningful when they are substantiated by the love of God. As new creatures in Christ, we should serve others with pure and proper intention. The spiritual sustainability of this exceptional form of love is explained by Paul in

---

[116] Matthew 25:35-40 (NET).

his letter to the Corinthians where he wrote, "Love never fails." [117]

Christians ought to love each other. We share similar interests in the things that matter most in this life. Our lives' purpose, our goals and ambitions, and all our hopes and dreams center on Jesus Christ. But this exceptional expression of love should not be restricted to just those of similar faith and feelings. We must not remain content in simply loving the Christian family alone. We have an obligation beyond the fold of Christ that reaches throughout the entire world, and we should be anxious to bless all of humanity.

We should develop a love for all people everywhere. Our hearts should reach out to everyone in the pure love of God.

Four Obstacles to Pure Love

Christian love is so vital to the sustainability of our spiritual selves that Satan works constantly at

---

[117] 1 Corinthians 13:8 (WEB).

setting up stumbling blocks and barriers to the practice of this spiritual gift. Things just seem to "get in the way" to prevent us from sharing the love of God with others. The following are some of the more common obstacles to pure love:

1. *Egocentricity.* When we become self-absorbed we cannot feel the pure love of Christ or effectively share it with other people. The love of God is not a love of personal gratification. Pure love pursues the joy and happiness of others. Christ's commission to "love your neighbor as yourself" [118] has little concern with loving ourselves; it's interest and focus is in loving others and exemplifying the Golden Rule taught by Jesus in the sermon at Galilee. [119] The irony of the gospel of Jesus Christ is that only by losing our life can we truly find it. [120]

2. *Deceitfulness.* By opening ourselves to the truth and living in harmony with that truth we can

---

[118] Matthew 19:19 (NET).
[119] See Matthew 7:12.
[120] See Matthew 16:25.

develop God-like love. In Dostoyevsky's classic work, The Brothers Karamazov, Zossima says to Feodor, "A man who lies to himself and who listens to his own lies gets to a point where he can't distinguish any truth in himself or in those around him, and so loses all respect for himself and for others. Having no respect for anyone, he ceases to love, and to occupy and distract himself without love he becomes a prey to his passions and gives himself up to coarse pleasures...and all this from continual lying to people and to himself." [121]

3. *Sin*. Wickedness weakens love and lust is a pitiful substitute for pure love. The love God bestows on us is a spiritual gift and it is given as a result of our faithfulness. Sin naturally prevents us from fully receiving and sharing this gift.

4. *Thoughtlessness*. When we characterize vulgar, cruel and uncaring language and behaviors, we offend and alienate the Holy Spirit. Man's inhumanity to man, whether in the form of

---

[121] Dostoyevsky, *The Brothers Karamazov*, p. 47.

viciousness and violence or simply sarcasm and insult, will, over time, desensitize us to the tender and sympathetic feelings that foster and encourage pure love.

Active and sincere love based in the teachings of Jesus of Nazareth is undoubtedly the greatest need in the world. But much of the world today rejects those teachings. Spiritual sustainability requires that sincere Christians proclaim the truth of Christ's teachings and demonstrate to everyone the power and peace of a righteous, gentle life.

Jesus counsels us to "love your enemies, bless them that curse you, do good to them that hate you, and pray for them which despitefully use you, and persecute you." [122] Imagine the change this one concept alone could create in our neighborhoods, our local communities and in the countries that comprise our great global family.

---

[122] Matthew 5:44 (KJV).

If loving our enemies seems like an unreasonable and unrealistic challenge, consider instead the dreadful, deadly challenges waged by war, posed by poverty, created by crime and all the piercing pain caused by these past solutions.

What should we do when someone we love hurts us? How should we react when we are treated unfairly? What happens within our hearts when we are lied to, treated unkindly, misunderstood or sinned against?

Should we fight back? Should we counter with an even larger barrage of offenses, insults and lies? Do we give an eye for an eye and a tooth for a tooth? Such solutions are far from sustainable and, as Tevye from *Fiddler on the Roof* suggests, in the end will only leave us blind and toothless.

What all these situations do provide is the possibility for us to practice our Christian values and lifestyle. They provide us an invaluable opportunity to forgive others their debts as we seek similar forgiveness from our Father. [123]

Jesus' message of love, as one writer so eloquently states, "flowed forth as sweetly and as lavishly to single listeners as to enraptured crowds; and some of its very richest revelations were vouchsafed, neither to rulers nor to multitudes, but to the persecuted outcast of the Jewish synagogue, to the timid inquirer in the lonely midnight, and the frail woman by the noonday well.

"His teachings dealt not so much with ceremony and minutia as with the human soul, and human destiny, and human life filled with faith and hope and charity.

"Springing from the depths of holy emotions, [his teachings] thrilled the being of every listener as with an electric flame.

"In a word, his authority was the authority of God. Christ's voice was pure and pervaded with

---

[123] See Matthew 6:12.

sympathy. Even the severity of his sternest injunctions was expressed with an unutterable love."[124]

God's pure love is the "more excellent way" [125] Paul described that constitutes one of the greatest gifts God has given us. Christians have an obligation to serve others [126] but service without love is no service at all. Christian love is the noblest form of love. It is a gift of the Spirit that elevates us to a level of increased kindness and compassion for others. We can serve without loving but we can't genuinely love without serving. If you want to reach out to God, try reaching out to some of his other children here on Earth.

Until we develop the sustaining power of a Christ-like love, we can render all the Christian service we want and never gain a deep-rooted, permanent and fully sustainable Christian character.

---

[124] Farrar, Frederic W., *The Life of Christ* [Portland, Oregon: Fountain Publications, 1964], 215.
[125] 1 Corinthians 12:31 (NET).
[126] See James 2:8.

Paul understood this. He cautioned against giving away our possessions to feed the poor if we are missing the Christ-like quality of pure love to back-up our intentions. [127] When we are imbued with pure love, we perform Christian service not because we think it's the right thing to do but because that is simply who we are.

Now that we have discussed the ideal of developing a sustainable God-like love, where do we go from here? We know that our service and deeds should be motivated by pure love, but what do we do if our motives fall short of our knowledge and expectation? We can still try to do what is right, even if our hearts are not fully invested. We can ask God to give substance and meaning to our actions. We can do the work and pray for purer motives and more righteous desires.

The Holy Spirit purifies and cleanses our hearts but it does much more than just empty out uncleanness. It also fills. It fills our hearts and souls

---

[127] See 1 Corinthians 13:3.

with a sincere desire to walk as Jesus walked, performing acts of kindness throughout our lives. When we are filled with the Holy Spirit and with pure God-like love, we embody goodness. We do not necessarily need to plan and plot and design our good deeds and Christian acts in every circumstance. Rather, our good works will arise automatically from our reborn nature and provide evidence of our commitment to Christ.

We can live in a world of turmoil and still be at peace. We can survive in a society that is steeped in anxiety and uncertainty and still feel at ease. We can be surrounded on all sides by people who are worried, frightened and alarmed, and still feel secure because "perfect love drives out fear." [128]

The pinnacle of spiritual sustainability is described by Paul in his letter to the people in Rome: "I am convinced that neither death, nor life, nor angels, nor heavenly rulers, nor things that are present, nor things to come, nor powers, nor height,

---

[128] 1 John 4:18 (NET).

201

nor depth, nor anything else in creation will be able to separate us from the love of God in Christ Jesus our Lord." [129]

Life can be filled with its fair share of fear and failure; it's days of discouragement and despair. Friends and family may forsake us. Situations and circumstances may often fall short and fail to meet our expectations and desires, leaving us with little strength to go on. And yes, with all of its hardship and heartache, life can leave us feeling very much alone.

But one thing will never fail us. One solitary thing will stand the test of all time, all tribulation, all trouble, and all transgression; and that is the pure love of Christ. The love of Christ will always see us through. It is Christ's love which is patient and kind; not envious or boasting. It is Christ's love which is not self-serving, not easily angered or resentful. His love enables us to bear all things, believe all things, hope all things, and endure all things. It is Christ's

---

[129] Romans 8:38, 39 (NET).

love which is fully sustainable because, as Paul explains, "Love never ends." [130] When other gifts of the Spirit falter or fail, the love of Christ will still burn brightly in the Christian heart. "When what is perfect comes," the faithful followers of Christ will become filled with his fully sustainable and everlasting love.

---

[130] 1 Corinthians 13:3 (NET).

CHAPTER TWELVE

SUSTAINABLE THROUGH THE STORMS

Eighty miles north of Jerusalem sits a resplendent lake known in biblical times as the Sea of Kinnereth or the Lake of Gennesaret. It is a freshwater lake about twelve miles long and seven miles wide that is fed by the Jordan River. Today, we refer to it as the Sea of Galilee.

The Sea of Galilee is the lake Jesus knew as a child. Its fertile western shore is situated about fifteen miles east of his hometown of Nazareth. The Sea of Galilee and the adjacent Galilean hills provided a refuse where Jesus could so often return during the arduous days of his ministry.

Jesus frequently taught crowds of faithful followers and interested by-standers along the shores of Galilee. As the crowds pushed against him, Jesus would climb into a boat and push out a few yards to sea. Remaining close to shore, the master Teacher could then be more easily seen and heard by those straining to catch his powerful instruction.

The Sea of Galilee is situated about 680 feet below sea level with hills that rise sharply against the sky. The peaceful calm of the sea can change quite unexpectedly. Winds that funnel through the Galilean hill country can suddenly stir up the waters, but the more severe winds off the Golan Heights can be deadly. Cold air rushing down from the hills meets the warmer air rising off the lake and creates sudden, fleeting storms with ten-foot-high waves on the surface of the sea.

On one such evening, Jesus, after imparting his message to the crowds, set out with his disciples toward the opposite shore of the lake. Mark described what happened when "a great windstorm developed and the waves were breaking into the boat, so that the boat was nearly swamped.

"But he was in the stern, sleeping on a cushion. They woke him up and said to him, 'Teacher, don't you care that we are about to die?'

"So he got up and rebuked the wind, and said to the sea, 'Be quiet! Calm down!' Then the wind stopped and it was dead calm.

"And he said to them, 'Why are you cowardly? Do you still not have faith?'

"They were overwhelmed with fear and said to one another, 'Who then is this? Even the wind and sea obey him!'" [131]

In Genesis, God commanded, "Let there be an expanse in the midst of the waters and let it separate water from water." [132] He also ordered "the water

---

[131] Mark 4:37-41 (NET).
[132] Genesis 1:6 (NET).

under the sky be gathered into one place and let dry ground appear. And it was so." [133] In Exodus, he parted the Red Sea, allowing the Israelites to cross over on dry ground. [134] It certainly shouldn't surprise us that Jesus could calm a simple storm on the Sea of Galilee.

We have all had sudden storms in our lives which seemingly appear out of nowhere. At times these temporary, fleeting storms can seem as devastating and frightening and potentially destructive as the storms of Galilee. In our personal lives, in our families, in our communities and even in our country, we have seen squalls arise that make us wonder, "Teacher, don't you care that we are about to die?" But always, in the stillness after the storm we sense somehow the words of the Master, "Why are you cowardly? Do you still not have faith?"

No one likes being called a coward and none of us would like to think that we don't have faith, but

---

[133] Genesis 1:9 (NET).
[134] See Exodus 14:21, 22.

Jesus' soft scolding may be slightly deserved. Our faith should be our reminder that Christ can calm the troubled seas of our lives as easily as he calmed the Sea of Galilee.

I am reasonably certain that we will all experience hardship and misfortune over the course of our lifetimes. It seems none of us is immune. Some difficulties may be brutal, cruel and potentially destructive. They could even make us question our faith in God.

But Jesus has pre-warned us that in this world we would "have trouble and suffering, but take courage – I have conquered the world." [135] He also promised: "Peace I leave with you; my peace I give to you. I do not give it to you as the world does. Do not let your hearts be distressed or lacking in courage."[136]

On another evening, Jesus' disciples set out on a voyage across the same Sea of Galilee. Again, the

---

[135] John 16:33 (NET).
[136] John 14:27 (NET).

wind became fierce and frightful, the waves bold and boisterous. The desperate disciples were worried because, this time, no one sailed with them who could calm the storm. Jesus had been left alone on the shore.

The boat was far from land and the violent waves and wind were beating against it. Suddenly, as the night was ending, the disciples perceived in the darkness a fluttering robe walking toward them on waves of the sea. Believing it was a phantom that moved on the water, terror struck at their hearts. But Jesus called to them through the tempest and the darkness—just as he so often calls to us when we feel closed off in obscurity and surrounded by the raging storms of life—with a reassuring and peaceful declaration, "Have courage! It is I. Do not be afraid."

Peter shouted, "Lord, if it is you, order me to come to you on the water." Jesus' simple answer to him was the same instruction he offers to all of us: "Come."

And so Peter climbed out of the boat and onto the turbulent sea. He must have been aware of the storm around him and felt the harsh waves splashing at his feet but while he kept his eyes fixed on the Savior, he was fine. When he removed his eyes from Christ and saw the dark and frightening waves beneath him, fear took hold and he started to sink.

Like us, when we are sinking into despair and drowning in our troubles, Peter called out, "Lord, save me!" Jesus immediately reached out his hand and caught the drowning disciple. "You of little faith," Jesus gently rebuked, "why did you doubt?" Safely back on board, the wind stopped, the rage became a ripple and the boat sailed on to the land of Gennesaret. [137]

Jesus is the one truly infallible light on the stormy sea of life. A light to the world, Jesus is the one unfailing beacon. He is "the way, the truth, and the life." [138] With our eyes fixed securely on him, we

---

[137] See Matthew 14:22-33.
[138] John 14:6 (KJV).

can walk safely over the waves of worry and despair. When we focus on the force and fierceness of the destructive influences around us, as we are so easily tempted to do in this world, we inevitably sink in a sea of conflict, sorrow, and hopelessness.

On the shore of peace and tranquility, Jesus Christ is the only dependable beacon on which we can firmly rely. When we feel the floods threatening to drown us and the waves eager to devour the tiny tossed vessel of our faith, during the darkest hours of our storm the comforting words of Christ resonate within our hearts: "Have courage! It is I. Do not be afraid." [139]

Sustaining Hope

After Moses gave the laws and the commandments to the ancient Israelites, the Lord told them, "Today I invoke heaven and earth as a witness against you that I have set life and death,

---

[139] Matthew 14:27 (NET).

blessing and curse, before you. Therefore, choose life so that you and your descendants may live!

"I also call on you to love the Lord your God, to obey him and be loyal to him, for he gives you life and enables you to live continually in the land the Lord promised to give to your ancestors Abraham, Isaac, and Jacob." [140]

The source of sustainable hope is the source of life.

Hope is one of the three great Christian virtues.

Hope will endure in the human heart even when all odds are against it. When our own knowledge, judgment and experience tell us there is no reason to hope, hope will persist.

To choose hope is to choose life. The choice offered by the Lord your God is life, and life offers hope. Hope in Christ offers hope in the future. Our

---

[140] Deuteronomy 30:19, 20 (NET).

ordinary, everyday hope can become so strong, so versatile and so sustainable that worthlessness and despair could not exist within us. When we choose Christ we literally cannot despair unless we consciously decide to do so.

Death may be entangled with life but we still choose to either feed darkness and death, or we choose to feed brightness and hope. We can choose to worry away our lives. We can refuse the light of Jesus Christ. Piece by piece, a little at a time, we can give our lives over to the devil until we no longer have the power to wrench them free again. We can strangle all our hopes until meaninglessness and despair overcome us. But it will always be a conscious choice.

Christ submitted himself to death but, "has been raised from the dead, he is never going to die again; death no longer has mastery over him." [141] Jesus is the master of life and the master over death. Any choice other than Christ is a choice of spiritual

---

[141] Romans 6:9 (NET).

death. Physical death has no power over him, and in the end will have no power over us through Christ.

Life and hope are always stronger than death. If we choose hope, we set in motion powerful spiritual forces for life. Jesus Christ responds to those tender tendrils of crippled life with the force and energy that will bring them to flowering.

We can choose hope in the depths of despair. We can choose growth in the midst of oppression. We can choose understanding in the presence of ignorance. We can choose love in the arms of violence and hatred. We can choose to forgive, to pray, to be kind, to help each other. When we do, we will feel Christ's abundant love. He sees every kindness to even the poorest human creature as a kindness to him. In exchange, he adds hope, strength, joy and meaning to our lives.

Paul asked, "Who will separate us from the love of Christ? Will trouble, or distress, or persecution, or famine, or nakedness, or danger, or sword?

"…. No, in all these things we have complete victory through him who loved us.

"For I am convinced that neither death, nor life, nor angels, nor heavenly rulers, nor things that are present, nor things to come, nor powers,

"nor height, nor depth, nor anything else in creation will be able to separate us from the love of God in Christ Jesus our Lord." [142]

Christ is our only sustainable hope. He is our hope during our darkest nights. He is our hope on those miserable Monday mornings. He is our hope when depression and despair darken our doorway. Jesus has declared, "I am the door. If anyone enters through me, he will be saved." [143] Despair is the thief of life. Depression comes only to steal, and to kill, and to destroy. But Jesus has come that we may have life, and that we may have it abundantly. He is the

---

[142] Romans 8:35-39 (NET).
[143] John 10:9 (NET).

good shepherd and he assures us, "The good shepherd lays down his life for the sheep." [144]

---

[144] See John 10:9-11.

CHAPTER THIRTEEN

RESILIENT SUSTAINABLE FAITH

In a sustainable ecology, resiliency refers to the capacity of an ecosystem to absorb disturbance and still retain its basic structure and viability. Resiliency-based thinking evolved from a need to manage interactions between human-built systems and natural ecosystems in a sustainable way. Resiliency addresses how much ecosystems can withstand the assault from human disturbances and still provide the services needed by current and future generations.

Any closed system that can maintain productivity by replacing human-spent resources with resources of equal or greater value without degrading or endangering the natural biotic system would be considered a viably sustainable system. Sustainability exists in human projects if expended resources are continually replaced in the ecosystem to replenish the depleted resources. This occurs naturally in nature through the process of adaptation as an ecosystem re-establishes its viability after an external disturbance. Adaptation is a process that begins with the disturbance event (earthquake, volcanic eruption, hurricane, tornado, flood, or thunderstorm), followed by absorption, utilization, or deflection of the energy created by the external forces.

When the disturbances in an ecosystem are created by human actions (urban and national parks, dams, farms and gardens, theme parks, open-pit mines, water catchments), then sustainability provides the long-term vision for adaptation while resiliency becomes the ability of human engineers to respond to the immediate environmental needs.

The Christian commitment and lifestyle also demand both the need for resiliency and the long-term vision of sustainability. Constancy and steadfastness are the criterion for all those who have come out of the world. We hear of plenty of Christians with remarkable conversion stories but who fail to remain true and faithful to the day-by-day constraints of Christian discipleship. Christ calls for more than just a flash-in-the-pan attempt at Christian living. When we have been born again and felt the sustaining, resilient power of the Spirit, we should still hunger and thirst after righteousness as we continue to cultivate the gifts of the Spirit.

One indication of spiritual sustainability and maturity is our responsive resolve to live a Christian lifestyle. As our faith becomes more resilient, we can respond more maturely to trials, temptations and the tragic events that will certainly surface in our lives.

The call of Christ to remain resilient to the end is fundamental to our faith. God doesn't just want starters; he wants finishers. He wants disciples who "compute the cost" and are willing to stay in the battle until its conclusion. [145] Having fully sustainable and resilient faith means we finish our Earthly existence in the faith and go to our eternal reward after this life. Sustainable and resilient faith requires living our lives, day-by-day, as Jesus wants us to live them.

Charles Sheldon's best-selling Christian classic, *In His Steps*, is a meaningful story about the challenges a Protestant minister faced when he determined to seriously attempt to emulate the example of the only sinless soul who ever walked on Earth. Before making any decision he resolved to ask himself, "What would Jesus do?" He invited his entire congregation to do the same.

How would a similar covenant affect our present lifestyles? Would it change the way we talk

---

[145] See Luke 14:25-33.

to our neighbors? Would it affect the type of entertainment we watch? Would it change what we view on the internet? How would it affect the way we do business or perform at our jobs? If we asked ourselves, "What would Jesus do?," would we have the courage to follow where he leads us?

We can learn how Jesus would act if we study his life and ministry in the New Testament, observing how he treated his friends, noticing how he handled his enemies, determining how he dealt with difficulties, reviewing how he regarded worship and adoration, perceiving how he preached the gospel. We learn how to act and re-act like Jesus when we study the Bible, a cherished collection of the words of Christ.

When we are born of the Spirit and earnestly seek Christ, we will become resilient in surmounting life's problems and perplexities. When we renounce the world and its enticements, we generate wisdom, judgment and confidence. Finding our sustainability in spirituality, we can then lift, enlighten and liberate others.

The Gift of Faith

Resilient, sustainable faith entails believing in Jesus Christ and accepting what the Bible says about him. It involves trusting in his redemptive power and relying solely on his merits, mercy, and grace for our salvation. Resilient, sustainable faith means we choose Christ and his gospel over everything else. As we mentioned earlier, Paul taught that "faith comes by hearing, and hearing by the word of God." [146]

Resilient faith requires discipline. We demonstrate resilient faith when we shun profanity, vulgarity, crudeness, and spiritual insensitivity. We exhibit resilient faith when we refuse to speak unkindly toward or about our fellow Christians. We show resilient faith through firmness, dependability, and stability in the cause of Christ. We display resilient faith when we surrender to Jesus, when we

---

[146] Romans 10:17 (WEB).

do what he has lovingly invited us to do and cast our burdens at his feet. [147]

Resilient, sustainable faith means that when we are in the middle of a personal crisis, financial frustration, unemployment, depression or spiritual drought, we refuse to succumb to our tragic circumstances but allow Jesus, instead, to do the caring, the struggling and the worrying for us. We evidence sustainable faith when we see the larger picture and live today in light of eternity.

The notion of faith is a universal, all-inclusive concept. Paul stated that "without faith it is impossible to please him, for the one who approaches God must believe that he exists and that he rewards those who seek him." [148] Why is it impossible to please God without faith? Because without faith it is impossible to be saved; and as God desires our salvation, he must, of course, desire that

---

[147] See 1 Peter 5:7, Matthew 11:28-30.
[148] Hebrews 11:6 (NET).

we have faith. Faith must clearly be at the center of all that we do.

Faith is a fascinating concept. What is faith? How does it work? Do we ever achieve complete and total faith? It would be difficult or perhaps even impossible to completely understand faith in our lifetime. Even the most scholarly, intellectual students of the Bible will never gain a complete knowledge of the workings of faith. The gospel of Christ is so simple yet so sophisticated that the greatest intellects can study faith and never completely understand it.

Resilient, sustainable faith is not an object but rather, a process. It is a process that involves various stages of development. At every stage of development, we experience a variety of faith factors before reaching the next level.

Stage One: Hope

Hope is the first step in the entire process of understanding and developing faith. Hope is simply a desire or a wish that something be true. It is nothing more than saying to ourselves, "I want to know if this is true." The great power of hope is that, if we have hope then we will be motivated to act. At first, this action is basically no more than a willingness to find out if what we have heard is true.

Paul taught us about this level of faith when he wrote, "Now faith is being sure of what we hope for, being convinced of what we do not see." [149] At this level, faith is the ability to trust in something we do not clearly see or understand. We cannot actually "see" that the words of the gospel are true. And although there is no empirical evidence or proof based on observation or experience, we have faith in the truthfulness of the word. And so we act on our faith; we trust or hope for something, although it is not yet based on any physical, demonstrable evidence.

At every level in the development of our faith, we will experience a test of our faith. We are tested

---

[149] Hebrews 11:1 (NET).

to see if we will act on the basis of our hope. We need to demonstrate that we are motivated to behave according to the faith God gives us before we can obtain actual evidence that these things are true. As we pass through this test of our faith, experiencing a measure of hope that encourages us to act, we will be given a validation of our hope. This is the first stage of faith.

It is essential that we act on our hope to know if the word of God is true. This initial level of action is basically deciding to try to find out if the word is true. As we investigate, stimulate, and implement, then we are given a substantiation of our hope. Although this evidence is available only as feelings, it is still empirical, real evidence. It may be difficult to put into words, but that doesn't make it any less real. Based on this difficult-to-express but real proof, our faith has now been substantiated by empirical evidence.

In this first stage we are acting like a spiritual private investigator. We are investigating whether or not something is true. When we honestly humble ourselves at hearing the word of God and make an investigation into it by seeking to know (for instance, through prayer) whether it is true, we experience the confirmation, the feeling of truthfulness, the almost indescribable sensation that this is good, and we know that the word of God is true.

Stage Two: Knowledge

Once our hopes have been realized, have we acquired all the faith that is available? Definitely not! Once we have hope, we can move on to the next echelon in the process of developing faith. The second stage of faith is a level which entails belief and knowledge. At this stage, we have more than just a desire to know if the word of God is true. Our attitude changes from, "I want to know if this is true," to something closer to, "I want this truth to be a part of how I live my life."

When we reach this second stage, we begin to sincerely believe in the things we have heard rather than simply desiring to believe. Once again, we are motivated to act. Our actions now are on a higher plane. They demonstrate a willingness to live the principles we believe to be true. Before we had simply acted to see if God's word was true. Now we act to incorporate the truths we learned into our daily lives. We begin to live like Christian disciples.

At this second stage, we again undertake a test of our faith. We still need to demonstrate that we are willing to trust in things not seen. As our belief becomes evident, we will again receive a validation of our faith. This empirical evidence will occur on a behavioral level. It is an outward confirmation that is more apparent than the evidence of inner feelings experienced at stage one. Stage two evidence is easier to identify and express in words. Stage two evidence involves our prayers being answered or witnessing how God blesses our lives when we obey his law. At stage two we move from "I believe in God" to "I know that God lives!"

Now we can begin to appreciate the profound implications of faith and works discussed by James.

It should be evident to us that if works do not accompany our faith, then our faith "is dead, being by itself." [150] On one level, if we hope that something is true but don't act on our hope, we will not obtain the desired evidence and our faith will be dead. On another level, if we believe something is true but refuse to live by that truth, then all we have is faith without works, and our faith dies. There will be no witness or evidence. Evidence only comes after our faith has been tested.

Stage Three: Power

The next stage of faith is the power level of faith. Our determination has moved from "I want to know if this is true" (stage one), to "I want this truth to be a part of how I live my life" (stage two), and is now manifested in the statement, "I have the truth, and I wish to use it in my life." When this becomes the strength of our hope and we have the knowledge and assurance of unseen things, then we become even more committed to act. At this stage of faith, we

---

[150] James 2:17 (NET).

are willing to do whatever God asks of us. This, again, is a test of our faith. It may involve simply helping a sick neighbor or volunteering on a project at church, or it could seem as great a sacrifice and challenge to us as God's request to Abraham that he sacrifice his only son.

If we reach this point of resilient, sustainable faith but refuse to act on it, then, we do not truly have faith. As James said, "just as the body without the spirit is dead, so also faith without works is dead." [151] If we fail to act, we fail the test of our faith and will receive no verification of our hope. Being willing to do whatever God asks will allow us to obtain resilient, sustainable faith.

The evidence that comes at this stage of faith will include inner feelings but will also comprise the physical senses, as in the manifestation of miracles. This is irrefutable evidence, evidence that any honest person cannot deny. This is the evidence Jesus

---

[151] James 2:26 (NET).

Christ promised the faithful when he said, "These signs shall accompany those who believe." [152]

This three-stage process of developing faith helps us understand why Jesus taught that "a wicked and adulterous generation asks for a sign." [153] When we try to build or bolster our faith on the basis of physical evidence alone, without living the laws and principles of the gospel, we sidestep the testing of our faith. We want proof without paying the price of hoping and acting. In this way we adulterate and pollute the proper procedure in the development of our faith. Circumventing the process in this way will never provide us with resilient, sustainable faith.

In 1 Corinthians, chapter 13, Paul teaches us how faith, hope, and love are all interlaced and inter-reliant concepts. We have seen the correlation of faith and hope throughout the three stages of sustainable faith development, but where does love come into play? Love is actually involved at every

---

[152] Mark 16:17 (NET).
[153] Matthew 16:4 (NET).

stage and every aspect of the development of resilient, sustainable faith. The love of Christ substantiates each stage of action and makes it successful, profitable and rewarding. Paul said that we can prophesy or give to the poor or do any number of other good deeds, but our actions would be meaningless without love.

Love lights our hope, reinforces our resolve, and deepens our determination. It is patient and tolerant. It is properly motivated. Love hopes for all things, and endures all things. Love permeates the entire process of developing sustainable faith. Love is the greatest of all because love never ends. Love is fully sustainable.

CHAPTER FOURTEEN

SPIRITUAL CYCLES AND SUSTAINABILITY

Have you ever noticed that our lives seem to rotate in cycles? Clocks turn in circles of seconds, minutes and hours. These in turn become days, weeks, months and years. We mark the end of a year with resolutions for a better, new year ahead. The Earth spins in circles as it also rotates around the sun. The seasons faithfully start and stop their cycles with uniformity.

One cycle that farmers are most familiar with is known as crop rotation. In order to develop sustainable farming, agriculturalists practice crop rotation (or crop sequencing) by alternating deep-rooted and shallow-rooted plants. This method of planting attempts to balance the fertility demands of various crops to avoid excessive depletion of soil nutrients and to improve soil structure and fertility.

We should approach our spiritual sustainability with the same wisdom we demand from our agriculturists and farmers. We should be equally concerned for tending what we plant in our hearts as we are about tending what we plant in our gardens.

We tend to live in cycles of spirituality as well. We drift from the course defined by Jesus Christ and disregard God's standards. Values and ideals that once characterized our life become clouded and uncertain and our behavior begins to reflect this beclouding of gospel doctrines. These un-spiritual practices deplete our inner spiritual soil. Our spirituality must be replenished through other spiritual practices.

We must apply the same principles and preparations of crop rotation to our spiritual practices as diligently as we do to our agronomy. The safest path to pursue is to stay firm to the standards set by God. Only within the gospel of Jesus Christ can we find a refuge from the evils of the world and when we come to Christ we need to commit completely.

In his book, *Mere Christianity*, C. S. Lewis explains that "Christ says, 'Give me All. I don't want so much of your time and so much of your money and so much of your work: I want You. I have not come to torment your natural self, but to kill it. No half-measures are any good. I don't want to cut off a branch here and a branch there, I want to have the whole tree down. I don't want to drill the tooth, or crown it, or stop it, but to have it out. Hand over the whole natural self, all the desires which you think innocent as well as the ones you think wicked—the whole outfit. I will give you a new self instead. In fact,

I will give you Myself: my own will shall become yours'." [154]

Our commitment to Christ and our commitment to living a spiritual life must be both internal and external; otherwise, it is not sustainable. The depth of our commitment and spirituality can be easily portrayed in nothing more and nothing less than our predisposition to do the right things for the right reasons.

Unfortunately, life allows for ample incongruence between genuine, authentic spirituality and a mere appearance and formality of Godliness. Our human failing creates a deceptive fraud to which anyone can fall victim. It's not that we don't value our commitment to Christ, it's just that we begin to take it for granted.

I once inherited an old Buick from my father. It wasn't the greatest car but it got me where I needed to go. The longer I drove that old car, the less

---

[154] Lewis, C.S., *Mere Christianity*, London: Collins, 1988, p. 167.

I seemed to appreciate it. I didn't really value that automobile until it broke down and I no longer had transportation. Some things we appreciate only when we no longer have them. Taking an automobile for granted is trivial compared to taking for granted our spiritual sustainability. Trivializing what is truly substantial while making false pretenses is an extremely dangerous self-deception.

For instance, we depreciate prayer when we reduce it from a sweet communion with God to rote repetition and a hollow echo of previously repeated petitions. We may often act as if prayer were meaningful by still getting down on our knees and offering the semblance of supplication but without any substance. The ruse remains in the conflict between outward appearances and inward substance, between our superficial fervor and our inner apathy.

Trivializing spiritual living impedes our possibility of cultivating legitimate spiritual sustainability. To reduce the risk of undervaluing our spiritual lives and activities, we need to maintain a proper perspective. If we view non-spiritual activities as spiritual and continue to offer God mere appearances and pretense, sustainable spirituality will elude us.

When we devalue genuine spirituality with a half-hearted devotion, we miss opportunities for real sustainable spiritual experiences. We sacrifice spiritual sustainability for empty form.

Of all of life's mockeries, nothing is imitated more often or counterfeited more frequently than spirituality. The world dishes up an unlimited buffet of tasteless vulgarities at the table of pretended religion. Everything from pompous piety to sickening obscenities pass for spiritual nutrition. Dishonesty and deception pose as truth. Sham and charade masquerade as genuine spirituality. Regardless of how appetizingly garnished, poisonous toadstools posing as spiritual mushrooms will eventually kill our divine nature.

Sustainable spirituality is not a sanctimonious list of "Thou shalts" and "Thou shalt nots."

Sustainable spirituality is not a gift of our time but a gift of ourselves.

Sustainable spirituality is not unrelenting vocal attacks imposing our tenets on the beliefs (or disbelieves) of other people.

Sustainable spirituality is not a religious rally or a bumper-sticker philosophy.

Sustainable spirituality is not the superficial motions of faithfulness but the deep devotion of discipleship.

Sustainable spirituality is not "if it feels good, do it" but "if it be your will, I'll do it."

Sustainable spirituality is not simply knowing the headlines and talking points of the gospel; it is not just talking of Christ but rejoicing in Christ.

Isaiah paints a beautiful picture to impress our minds and hearts with the ideal image of what sustainable spirituality is and how it is achieved:

"The work of righteousness shall be peace; and the effect of righteousness, quietness and confidence forever." [155]

God intended that our good works be done quietly and without fanfare. Audacious displays alienate his Spirit. His resultant spiritual rewards will also be inconspicuous. God is not a showman. Loud and undignified performances provide a poor alternative to the quiet confidence Isaiah portrays as sustainable spirituality.

Substance is necessary to sustainable spirituality, but sometimes even our substance becomes motivated by a non-spiritual intention. Ulterior motives in our behavior do not qualify as spiritual substance. For instance, sustainable

---

[155] Isaiah 32:17 (WEB).

spirituality is not motivated out of fear or to please and placate others based on what they might think.

Sustainable spirituality is not an avoidance of other personal responsibilities. Increasing what appears to be spiritual activity as a means of avoiding responsibility elsewhere is not true faithfulness or devotion. A man who dedicates his life to Christ while neglecting his family is not serving God; he is serving himself.

Sustainable spirituality is not performed at the expense of others. A woman who fosters guilt in her husband because he won't participate in family prayer is making prayer a weapon in her power struggle instead of a channel of communication with God.

Sustainable spirituality is not based on a need to dominate, control, and subjugate others. A man who uses his supposed spiritual nature to harass his wife and children is not motivated by a true spiritual intent.

Sustainable spirituality is not driven by a desire for personal recognition or reward. Christian service offered in exchange for praise or esteem is a false perception of spiritual service.

Cultivating sustainable spirituality can be extremely difficult because it runs contrary to our human nature. Finding God, undertaking a radical change of heart, and then committing ourselves to Christ is an arduous task. When we compound that with our tendency to trivialize the spiritual aspect of our lives, the development of sustainable spirituality can seem not only difficult but near impossible.

But the difficulty really lies in our perception. Sometimes spirituality is seen as a conquest. It is not something we earn and receive like a paycheck or a trophy we place on our mantel after reaching the finish line in a race. For spirituality to be sustainable it must be a process of training and development; an exercise to build the strength of our faith. Sustainable spirituality is not achieved by crossing a finish line but by participating in the race.

Our accomplishments are never as important as the righteousness and respectability that directs us in doing them. When we exemplify Christ, our spiritual nature becomes embedded in everything we do; in every choice we make, in every relationship we nurture, and in every insignificant act that comprises the substance of our living and lifestyle. Sustainable spirituality is not something we add to a long list of daily to-do's; it is the pattern that directs our doing. In other words, what we do is not nearly as important as how we do it.

A system of spiritual beliefs rooted in acts of righteousness, like a tree whose roots reach deep into the Earth, becomes impervious to being uprooted by the ideological storms and philosophical winds of human thinking. As Jesus explained, we can know the gospel only to the extent that we live it. [156]

Our faith is different from the world's; our actions should also be different from the world's.

---

[156] See John 7:17.

Faith-based action will develop our spirituality. If our actions and intents are commendable, our faith will also be commendable.

Spiritual sustainability requires effort. The development of spiritual sensitivity is a time-involved process. As we move through that process, what we experience today will work to our advantage tomorrow. The more we learn, the greater our capacity to learn. Spiritual practices are not mastered in a few simple attempts. It may take days, weeks, or even months.

People commonly compensate for the loss of a physical sense by an increased development of their other senses. The ability to develop and use these other senses was always there. It simply remained dormant until needed. Within each one of us exists a large number of latent spiritual senses anxiously waiting for us to develop them. When we become "partakers of the divine nature," [157]

---

[157] See 2 Peter 1:4.

sustainable spirituality and increased faith become the results of our everyday living.

Christ is the beacon that lights the path we walk. Our responsibility as disciples of Christ is to learn God's will for us and to do it. Our Christian obligation is not a crown we place on our heads but a tool we take up in our hands. The Christian pathway advances us from good deeds to great deeds, from life challenges to even greater life challenges, from simple service to extraordinary service. It carries us from hope to faith and from faith to power. Sustainable spirituality is worship in work clothes.

Peter advises us to "make every effort to be sure of your calling and election. For by doing this you will never stumble into sin. For thus an entrance into the eternal kingdom of our Lord and Savior, Jesus Christ, will be richly provided for you." [158]

---

[158] 2 Peter 1:10, 11 (NET).

CHAPTER FIFTEEN

SPIRITUAL MEANING AND PURPOSE

How do you live life filled with purpose?

If you have a specific goal to accomplish, an objective in life to work towards, you can certainly live with the distinct purpose of achieving that goal. But when you have reached your objective, what becomes of your purpose?

Living a life filled with purpose is much more than merely accomplishing a set goal for ourselves. Living with purpose means we live every moment of our life with intention. As Christians, our intention should always be spiritual. Our purpose should be to express spirituality in everything we do.

Living with purpose means infusing spiritual virtues into the mundane activities of daily living. It is about purposefully accessing the spiritual qualities innate within us. When we consciously take the time to live with a higher sense of spiritual purpose, God blesses our lives. This is a very powerful way to live.

Sustainable spirituality can become the basis of our entire existence. Spirituality empowers us to discover deeper meaning, purpose and value in our daily living. Spirituality stimulates us and provides us with a source of energy to sustain us through the difficulties of human existence.

Today's approach to spirituality is often individualistic. We see it as a sort of private enterprise that makes us, as individuals, feel peaceful, serene, and complete. New Age Spirituality is inwardly poised to keep me feeling whole and in my personal comfort zone. This type of pseudo-spirituality is individualistic in nature and shuts us off from the human family while drawing us into a state of self-absorption. Even in Christianity, the concept of "Jesus saved me but he hasn't saved you" can create a division in our connection with the rest of humanity. But Jesus tells us to love our neighbor as our self. [159] Sustainable spirituality draws us beyond self to a purpose of love and compassion for others.

Sustainable spirituality enables us to live with a sense of harmony with self. This inner harmonization becomes the basis of our way of living. But sustainable spirituality encompasses much more than self. It stimulates a response within us to live in harmony with others also on this planet. Authentic spirituality essentially sustains the life of the individual and the life of the planet through movements of compassion toward all people.

The development of sustainable spirituality draws us toward living with compassion so that all people on this planet may be sustained. Sustainable

---

[159] See Matthew 19:19.

spirituality creates an understanding of the underlying connection between the spiritual practice which provides meaning and purpose in our lives and the rest of humanity. Sustainable spiritual practices offer us a deep inner conviction as well as an encompassing compassion for all of God's other children on Earth. This compassion is demonstrated in concrete Christian service and action.

Sustainable spirituality recognizes a deep bond between the people on this planet and understands that all life is worthy of reverence. It allows us to live healthy, harmonious lives on Earth, respecting the inter-connected life of the planet and provides a sense for understanding the fundamental foundation that we are all children of God.

Living with spiritual meaning and purpose requires that we nourish our spirits. Each of us has a spirit that is the counterpart of our physical body. If we want to maintain a healthy and vigorous physical body, we must provide it with proper and adequate nutrition and exercise. Every cell of our bodies has a nerve connection necessary to maintain life. Without these nerve connections and the required supply of sustenance and nutrition, our bodies become susceptible to sickness, decay and death.

Our spirits also require sustenance to maintain their health and strength. Spiritual nourishment must come from spiritual sources. Feasting on eternal principles of truth from the Holy Scriptures and engaging in regular, frequent exercise in spiritual activities are absolutely essential to sustaining our spiritual strength and vitality. Sustainable spirituality can only be maintained through a sound connection with divine truth. Without a strong connection to our spiritual nerve center, our Savior Jesus Christ, we become susceptible to spiritual sickness, decay and death.

Each human being has five sides: A physical side, an intellectual side, a social side, an emotional side and a spiritual side. We go to great lengths to train and develop our physical side through regular and, hopefully, healthy feeding and daily exercise of one kind or another. We spend a good portion of our lives developing the intellectual side with schooling, college, training, and other forms of education. We invest countless hours in developing our social and emotional sides with friends and family.

We should develop our spiritual side with same amount of attention, care and curiosity. We should exercise our faith in prayer and in performing good deeds. We should feed our spirits the vital nutrition found in reading the Bible. We must stop feasting on the unhealthy concoctions being served up at Satan's buffet. Breaking God's commandments is as harmful to our spiritual self as drinking poison is to the physical self.

Living the gospel of Jesus Christ is the only way to sustain our spirituality and fully develop our spiritual side.

Anything worthwhile requires effort and sacrifice. Eternal blessings are founded on the basis of eternal truth. Just as a physical exercise program that costs us little effort will provide only minimal results, our spiritual exercise should not support laziness, lust or selfish desires and motives. We must not think to give as little as possible and still gain a great reward. We cannot expect a ton of miracles in exchange for an ounce of prayer. The wondrous and worthwhile blessings of our loving God are the result of conscientious and persistent effort.

Eternal Vigilance

The maxim of the last days is "preparation." As we walk the Christian pathway we must be certain that our feet have been fit "with the preparation that comes from the good news of peace." [160] Paul's personal experiences in living the gospel taught him that truth. He recognized that preparedness is the only guarantee for success. "Eternal vigilance," it has been said, "is the price of safety." Sustainable spirituality is the prized possession of those who are prepared.

---

[160] Ephesians 6:15 (NET).

Almost is a miserable word. When Paul gave his powerful witness before King Agrippa, the king replied, "Almost thou persuadest me to be a Christian." [161] King Agrippa recognized the eternal truth of Paul's preaching but he didn't have the faith or the courage to do what was required to become a Christian. Unfortunately, he was only *almost* persuaded. We may scoff at his lack of commitment but how many of us, under certain circumstances, are only *almost* persuaded to do what Jesus requires us to do?

In answering Christ's invitation to "Come, follow me," [162] some Christians are only almost persuaded. Our responses are similar to King Agrippa's:

"I'm almost persuaded to love my neighbor, but he's such a jerk!"

---

[161] Acts 26:28 (KJV).
[162] Mark 10:21 (NET).

"I'm almost persuaded to return the wallet I found, but no one has ever given back anything I lost."

"I'm almost persuaded to be honest and not cheat, but I really need an 'A' on this exam."

"I'm almost persuaded to go to church this Sunday, but the Pastor is so boring!"

"I'm almost persuaded to be tolerant of others' beliefs, but they're just so wrong."

"I'm almost persuaded to be forgiving, but the car in front of me should never have cut me off."

"I'm almost persuaded to pay my tithes, but I really want a new IPhone®."

Always almost! But not quite.

Imagine Jesus Christ making a similar commitment to us.

"I was almost persuaded to answer your prayer, but you always ask for so much."

"I was almost persuaded to forgive your wrong-doings, but your sins are just too shameful."

"I was almost persuaded to die for you, but those nails looked so painful."

Fortunately, every person "almost persuaded" can still come around and make a new start. Our lives are filled with new days and new beginnings. As we overcome our fears and gather faith and courage, we can build a sustainable level of spirituality. Any day we choose to try again, to make a renewed attempt to follow Christ, is a day we can draw strength from Jesus' promise that "nothing will be impossible." [163]

---

[163] Luke 1:37 (NET).

CHAPTER SIXTEEN

PERSONAL SUSTAINABILITY

With the promised prospect of trying and turbulent times ahead, we must remain informed about what is happening in the world today. But our modern-day, instantaneous communication systems can fill our homes and hearts with a drowning deluge of violence, suffering and deprivation. To maintain a level of sustainable spirituality, we need a time for peaceful spiritual renewal. We need to find the healing influence that brings solace to the soul.

In a world plagued with poverty, torn apart by terrorism, and steeped in sin, where can we find the recompensing relief so desperately needed to help us survive life's pressures? The counterbalancing comfort and spiritual restoring will, in large measure, come through increased communion with the Spirit of God.

We watch as the price of oil, gold, and other precious minerals increase daily. They may be beneficial and even essential to our current lifestyles, but they are also only material riches. They are the treasures we discover when we look down. We discover even greater treasures than these when we raise our vision and look up. We can discover intangible riches which come from pursuing and practicing sustainable spirituality.

Stephen, the first Christian martyr, "full of the Holy Spirit, looked intently toward heaven and saw the glory of God, and Jesus standing at the right hand of God." [164] The Spirit of God offers peace to our souls.

Spiritual Sustainability through Jesus

Jesus Christ is the Son of God, the most magnificent person who ever lived on this earth. The Bible outlines the many wondrous miracles he performed; turning water into wine, walking on water, calming a violent storm, healing the sick, restoring sight to the blind, even restoring life to the dead. Some people believe that Jesus was simply born with these great gifts and powers by virtue of his divine birthright. He was, after all, the Son of God. I believe that, despite his great spiritual capacity, even the Son of God had to discipline his thoughts and actions in the same way any of us must do.

Jesus was the Son of God but he still had to keep the commandments and be sinless to save the world from sin. He had power over death and yet, he

---

[164] Acts 7:55 (NET).

was mortal and could understand the pull and attraction of sin. Even Christ fought against the drawbacks of humanity. He was fully successful in winning the battle, but the Bible reveals that it was not always an easy struggle. Paul wrote, "He took not on him the nature of angels; but he took on him the seed of Abraham." [165]

Jesus was not born with a protective shield surrounding him that would preserve him from pain and sorrow and temptation. This divine Son of God was open to all the tender feelings, warmth, concern, and sensitivity shared by all of humanity. "Therefore he had to be made like his brothers and sisters in every respect, so that he could become a merciful and faithful high priest in things relating to God, to make atonement for the sins of the people. For since he himself suffered when he was tempted, he is able to help those who are tempted." [166] Paul also wrote that Jesus "has been tempted in every way just as we

---

[165] Hebrews 2:16 (KJV).
[166] Hebrews 2:17, 18 (NET).

are, yet without sin. Therefore let us confidently approach the throne of grace to receive mercy and find grace whenever we need help." [167]

Isaiah explained that the Messiah would be "despised and rejected...one who experienced pain and was acquainted with illness...treated harshly and afflicted." [168] Jesus knew more, felt more, understood more, suffered more, and was tempted more than any other person; but he remained obedient to God.

Jesus tells us that, "The one who sent me is with me. He has not left me alone, because I always do those things that please him." [169] Jesus gained sustainable spirituality from God and we can gain the same sustainable spirituality from Jesus. Jesus renounced the habits and lifestyles that his mortal nature may have desired and yet were wrong for him; and he became spiritually strong as a result of that

---

[167] Hebrews 4:15, 16 (NET).
[168] Isaiah 53:3, 7 (NET).
[169] John 8:29 (NET).

denial. With vivid and imaginative description, he said that we should renounce ourselves and take up the cross and follow him. [170]

Jesus' spiritual sustainability permitted him to do "everything well" [171] and to fulfill his mission and purpose with determination, tenderness and love. It sustained him to the end as he tread the winepress of redemption alone.

Evidences of the achievement of self-mastery in Jesus' life are found throughout the New Testament. Jesus gained spiritual strength through obedience and prayer. Jesus' spiritual strength came as a result of his triumphant struggles over the drag of humanity. His development and achievement of sustainable spiritual power came through his deliberate effort and by strength given to him from his Father.

Jesus' strength was in his absolute obedience and dedication to his Father's will. He did not

---

[170] See Matthew 16:24.
[171] Mark 7:37 (NET).

deviate or stray from the path of obedience. His ability to save the world required he be completely sinless and absolute in his self-denial and self-mastery. Jesus provided us our salvation, paying the highest price imaginable, the sacrifice of his own life. Jesus Christ, through his voluntary atoning sacrifice, "purchased [us] with his own blood." [172]

Jesus' life on Earth was destined to be difficult from the beginning. Satan saw to that. He influenced Herod the Great in his attempt to kill baby Jesus. After Jesus' baptism Satan attempted to overpower the Savior. He tried to make Jesus doubt his divinity and purpose. He tried to buy Jesus' allegiance by offering him the riches of the world.

As the Second Coming of Christ grows closer, we will experience increasing evidence of Satan's power. The opposition will be subtler and more exposed. It will be cunningly crafty, blatantly bold and disguised in superior sophistication. We will

---

[172] Acts 20:28 (WEB).

require increased sustainable spirituality and strength to resist it.

C. S. Lewis gives us alarming insight into Satan's devilish tactics in his book, *The Screwtape Letters*. In a fictional letter, Screwtape, a master devil, instructs his nephew Wormwood, an apprentice devil:

"You will say that these are very small sins; and doubtless, like all young tempters, you are anxious to be able to report spectacular wickedness.... It does not matter how small the sins are, provided that their cumulative effect is to edge the man away from the Light and out into the Nothing." [173]

Satan has experienced increased success. Hosts of humanity are being victimized by him and his angels. The shield against his onslaught is increased sustainable spirituality. Satan's attacks can be prevented by obedience to Christ and his

---

[173] Lewis, C.S., *The Screwtape Letters*, New York: Macmillan, 1961, pp. 64-65.

gospel. We must not be deceived by the devil. Satan does not sustain. He does not bless and elevate. He leaves his followers engulfed in shame and misery.

Only the Spirit of God is a sustaining and uplifting force and influence in our lives.

We must dedicate our lives to serving God and stop worrying about offending the devil. God will pardon our faults, our flaws and our frailties, and generously forgive our misdeeds as we repent and earnestly seek him.

Ups and Downs

Life has its ups and downs. One day brings happiness, another fills us with sadness and sorrow. We make elaborate plans, then abandon them as we head out in a different and unexpected direction. Some of God's blessings don't quite feel like blessings. He humbles our hearts, perfects our patience and fortifies our faith. Suffering somehow makes saints out of sinners as we learn tolerance, forgiveness, and self-mastery.

Cervantes' great masterpiece, *Don Quixote*, reminds us that where one door closes, another opens. Doors continually close in our lives, sometimes causing us severe pain and hardship. But where one door closes, another can open to fill us with hope and blessings that we may not have otherwise discovered.

None of us crave suffering. We avoid pain at all cost. But we also understand that Earth is a crucible of adversity and affliction. God's plan is to refine his children like silver in the refiner's fire. Jesus himself was not exempt from suffering. The suffering he endured was so intense that "his sweat became like great drops of blood falling down on the ground." [174]

All of us will, in one form or another, experience hardship and misfortune. The common plight of humanity is the experience of adversity, suffering, sickness, or other difficulties. Life can seem strenuous and unreasonably hard and

---

[174] Luke 44:22 (WEB).

challenging. Our faith is constantly tried and tested. It may even seem at times that God is punishing us. But the pain we experience, the trials we undertake are never wasted opportunities. They will increase our spiritual education and help us develop patience, faith, fortitude and humility. Life's trials will help us build our characters, purify our hearts, enlarge our souls, and make us kinder and more caring children of God.

Acres of beautiful roses grow in the little town of Roselandia, Brazil. You can stand on a small hill above the rose fields and witness their spectacular beauty and pleasant aroma. The sight and smell are breathtaking even though the rose bushes are covered with sharp, piercing thorns.

We must not allow the thorns and thistles of our lives to destroy the beautiful perspective we could enjoy by stepping back for a moment to concentrate on the beauty of life. We need to deal with the thorns but delight in the scent and splendor of the blossoms. As we attempt to live disciplined

Christian lives, reading scripture, praying, and obeying God, we will be able to savor the sweet aroma of God's blessings. The thorns will still be there, but they are only incidental to the sweet fragrances and exquisite beauty of the life God wants for us.

We should remember that where one door shuts, another opens. We cannot always see all the possible entries and exits. The mansion that God prepares for us may have particular passageways and deliberate doorways that he wants us to go through on our way to possess it.

At various and repeated times throughout our lives, we will have to accept that God knows what we do not know and sees what we do not see. "Indeed, my plans are not like your plans, and my deeds are not like your deeds." [175] When we have a problem, we may give God a list of what we think his possible

---

[175] Isaiah 55:8 (NET).

action plan might be in answering us, but he is not limited to our thinking.

Trust in the Lord

Peter had spent an entire night fishing without catching anything. Jesus told him to "Put out into deep water and lower your nets for a catch." Peter was an experienced fisherman. This was his livelihood and career. He had grown up on the Sea of Galilee. He knew about currents, the feeding habits of fish, and the best times to catch fish. Jesus was a carpenter. What did he know about fishing? Peter tried to explain to Jesus, respectfully but candidly, that they had been fishing all night and caught nothing! Jesus listened patiently as Peter discussed the facts of fishing. (And they were, after all, facts.) And when Peter was sure that Jesus, a carpenter, hadn't accidentally overlooked any of the facts important to a fisherman, he told Jesus, "At your word, I will lower the nets." Peter must have had enough spiritual experience with Jesus to know that there was something beyond material reality to consider. He did as the carpenter had instructed and he caught so many fish that the nets began to tear. [176]

Proverbs tells us to "trust in the Lord will all your heart, and do not rely on your own understanding." [177] We can trust our Savior in a way that we can trust no other living being.

Even the best human relationship is limited. We can't always trust our friends to be there when we need them. We can't always trust our mothers to be there when trouble shows up. We can't always trust our spouses to sense when we are lonely or sad. But we can always trust that Christ will be there and he will know what to do.

He will not always solve our problems for us, but he will be with us while we deal with them. He will sustain us spiritually by giving us the courage, the love, and the peace that we need to keep on going.

---

[176] See Luke 5:5, 6.
[177] Proverbs 3:5 (NET).

To be spiritually sustainable, we need to establish a deep and abiding relationship with the Lord Jesus Christ. He is always there and we can and should reach out to him.

He answers prayers.

He offers hope.

He provides peace.

"He is my refuge and my fortress: my God; in him will I trust." [178]

To be spiritually sustainable, we cannot depend on someone else's faith in Jesus. We can't expect someone else to get answers to our prayers. We can't ask someone else to listen to the whisperings of the Holy Spirit for us. We have to do it ourselves. We each have to carry our own oil for our own lamps.

To be spiritually sustainable, we need to realize our own inner strength that, with God's help,

---

[178] Psalm 91:2 (KJV).

we are "able to do all things through the one who strengthens" us. [179]

Unfortunately, Earth is not a vacation spot for the redeemed. It is more of a hospital for the hurt and ailing. Our life here is an encounter with failures as well as successes. We experience pain in our physical bodies. We become tired. We are weighed down with the demands of work and family. We are troubled over the animosity of neighbors. We face unexpected financial crises as bills continue to pile up. All of this suffering and frustration comes through our physical senses.

Sustainable spirituality does not deny these realities or pretend that they are unimportant. Instead, sustainable spirituality allows us to go faithfully forward in spite of these heart-rending realities. The purpose of sustainable spirituality is not to provide us a problem-free life. The purpose of

---

[179] Philippians 4:13 (NET).

sustainable spirituality is salvation through our Savior Jesus Christ.

Jesus is the only individual we can completely trust because he is the only one who has the power to keep all his promises and the only one who has the ability to act always out of love without ulterior motives. Sustainable spiritually means emulating Christ.

The kind and compassionate apostle John intertwined truth and love when he penned this poignant epistle to a nameless woman and her children:

"From the elder, to an elect lady and her children, whom I love in truth (and not I alone, but also all those who know the truth),

"because of the truth that resides in us and will be with us forever.

"Grace, mercy, and peace will be with us from God the Father and from Jesus Christ the Son of the Father, in truth and love." [180]

I pray the same blessings on all of you as you trust in Christ, approach him with pure hearts, speak the truth in love, and devote your efforts to building sustainable spirituality that will carry you through the toughest tribulation and trials and bring you peace and happiness in this world and eternal glory in the world to come.

May our hearts trust in him, and may we have his perfect peace as we live in truth and in love.

---

[180] 2 John 1:1-3 (NET).

ABOUT THE AUTHOR

Rich Nelson is the author of *The Powerful Christian Series*, seven books designed to bring the Power of God in greater abundance into our lives.

He has also written a variety of published articles on topics such as religious education, family values, health, and politics. His work has appeared in *Christian Education Today, Church Teacher, Parish Teacher, Living with Teenagers, Liberty Magazine,* and many others.

Contact Information:
Broken Hill Publications
Glenwood Springs, CO 91601

Email Rich at: rich@srnelson.com
Visit Rich at: www.srnelson.com

BOOKS BY S. RICHARD NELSON

Turning Faith into Power

Book 1 in The Powerful Christian Series.

Turning Faith into Power is the first in a series of instructive and inspirational books from The Powerful Christian Series by S. Richard Nelson. The Savior says in Matthew 17:19-20, "For most assuredly I tell you, If you have faith as a grain of mustard seed, you will tell this mountain, move from here to there, and it will move; and nothing will be impossible to you."

What mountains would you remove from your life if you had the faith of a mustard seed?

What's stopping you from removing the obstacles in your life?

Do you utilize your faith as a principle of action and power?

Is your faith centered where it will be most effective?

Do you have adequate faith in yourself?

As believing Christians there is substantial power available to us. It is the power of faith. Through the bounteous mercy and love of Jesus Christ we receive his grace—a divine means of strength. The power available to us through Jesus Christ is very real.

Gaining Power through Prayer

Book 2 in The Powerful Christian Series

Sincere prayer is a fountain of divine power flowing into our lives. Through prayer we gain clear and precise direction. Through prayer we access the strength of character to perform God's will—to do what is right. Prayer is the process we use to place ourselves in contact with God.

The impressive power of prayer warrants the consideration not only of Christians, but of all societies. This little booklet highlights the principle applications and purposes of prayer. It confirms that God does answer our prayers and demonstrates how we can be more aware of those divine answers. It also examines the challenging question of why, at times, it appears that God does not answer us and what we can do about it.

The Added Power of Obedience

Book 3 in The Powerful Christian Series

One of the most pronounced sources of spiritual power is obedience to the laws of God. Many are more than willing to die for their beliefs than to faithfully live them. The most effective way to introduce others to the word of God is not to die for it, but simply to obey it.

When God sends us a miracle, it is because we obeyed a commandment that justified a miracle. Any desire we hope to achieve or accomplish that is exceptional, substantial, or advantageous will be realized through obedience to God's law.

www.ingramcontent.com/pod-product-compliance
Lightning Source LLC
Chambersburg PA
CBHW070343090426
42733CB00009B/1270